Beyond the Bricks

by Daron Crawford and Pernell Russell

Neighborhood Story Project

P.O. Box 19742

New Orleans, LA 70179

www.neighborhoodstoryproject.org

Editor: Rachel Breunlin

Publisher: Abram Himelstein

Graphic Designer: Gareth Breunlin

The printing of this book made possible by
a generous grant from the Lupin Foundation.

THE
LUPIN
FOUNDATION

ISBN-13: 978-1-60801-016-5

Library of Congress Control Number: 2009940213

http://unopress.uno.edu

Dedication

I dedicate this book to my family for supporting me and being there for me when I needed them the most.

-Daron

I dedicate this book to Brandon Dugars, may he rest in peace. For being there for me as I was growing up and giving me positive advice to always stay focused and do the right thing.

I also dedicate this book to my mother for being my backbone when I needed you most, and just raising me into the person I am. I love you, Mama.

-Pernell

Daron's Acknowledgements

Thank-you

To my mom for giving me the life that I have and teaching me right from wrong.

To my dad for stepping up to the plate and taking on responsibility of taking care of my sister and me.

To Abram and Rachel for giving me the opportunity to express myself through this book.

To Rasta Doo for writing this book with me. I really appreciate the support you gave me along the way.

To Lea and Lindsey for taking great photos and helping with the best interviews.

To Kenneth, Susan, and Kareem for being right by my side during this whole book writing process.

To John McDonogh for making this class possible.

To Ms. Washington for pushing me to go to class so that I could finish this book.

To my uncle for going through the things you have been through and still being able to give positive advice.

To my book committee: Brittany, Matt, Willie, and Chevy Earnhard. Thanks for showing so much support. And to Brother Rob for helping me open up my eyes to life.

To my sister for helping me become a great writer and hoping one day you have your own book.

To my brother—stay focused in school so that you can be the best you can be. And for being such a pain in the butt. LOL

To the Freshstars for giving me lots and lots of motivation.

To Charmaine Spellman for helping me open up to express myself.

To my grandmother for bringing my mother to this world.

Special thanks to Shelley Price for showing so much love and support.

To my aunts for being there for me as a kid.

To Aunt Shanel—stay strong and keep your head up. I love you for being INDEPENDENT.

To Aunt Tasha—thanks for the love and support.

To everybody who donated money to help our book get published.

To T.I. for giving me motivation musically and staying focused on the things that I love most.

And most of all to God, for giving me life and putting me through the struggles I have been through to become a better man. I love you.

Pernell's Acknowledgements

Thanks to my mother for giving me life and raising me into the person I am, and just for being there for the Rasta. I love you, Mama.

Thanks to Rachel and Abram for making this possible for me. Without them I wouldn't have made it as far as I am now. They just never gave up on me.

Thanks to Fresh Star Money for writing this book with me.

Thanks to Lea and Lindsey for coming with me on my interviews and helping me with photos for our book.

Thank you to Aubrey Edwards for the awesome photo shoot at the Chat Room.

I want to thank everyone who has done something to help out the Neighborhood Story Project, even if you just stopped by.

I want to thank everyone for their great interviews—Javae for showing me how to dance, Roi Lowrey for being the best cousin you could have been, my daddy, my mama for your amazing story, Stephen for that great interview (thanks for the skateboard), Big Ed for helping me pull through when times got hard, and DJ D-Boi for being a good friend.

I want to thank Susan, Kareem, and Kenneth for being in the class with me, being good friends, and pushing. A special thanks to Susan for being there when I needed someone to talk to and for keeping it real.

I want to thank the Sigel St. for being a part of this—T-Tiga, Block, Roi Lowrey, Raheem Fresh, Hank, Keven, Rasta Doo, Three, EBBIE Cake, Caygoonie, and everyone else.

I also want to thank the city of New Orleans, from uptown to downtown—I mean the whole city. Without y'all, none of these stories would be possible.

I want to thank Lou Killa, Quann my sis, Snoop my far sis, Lova Girl Holly, BBG, Nee Rasta, Rasta DEE, Rasta Dua, Rasta Vae, Minnie, D-Boi. Thank you guys for believing in me.

I want to thank my book committee Willie, Brittany, Matt, and Markauise. Thank y'all for the good advice.

I also want to thank Brother Rob for being the best teacher in the world, and when I say "world," I mean it. For not giving up on me and Daron's book, and just being a part of it—that means a lot to us.

Table of Contents

Introduction

Daron = $ (handwritten)

Daron: When I say "Money," you might think I'm talking about the all-mighty dollar, but I'm talking about the young black dude who loves poppin his colla. Yes, you all know, it's me I'm talking about. People ask, "Why do you call yourself Money?" I tell them because money is one of the only reasons why I am in the rap game. The other reason is because I love doing what I do. When people call me Daron, I say, "That's not my name anymore." People act sarcastic and say, "I mean, Money." I have all the little kids in the neighborhood calling me Money. When I get out of the car, they all say, "What's up, Money?" It might sound funny, but to me, it makes me feel famous.

I grew up in the B.W. Cooper Housing Development in Uptown, New Orleans. We call it by its old name, the Calliope. The Calliope was known for rap because No Limit Records began there. People all over the country saw our project on Master P, C-Murder, and Silkk the Shocker videos. After Katrina, the project didn't reopen so my family moved into a house in New Orleans East and I started high school downtown at John McDonogh Senior High.

Pernell: My name is Pernell, which makes people think about lawyers and judges. I usually go by my nickname, Doo. I got both names from my father. I'm not your average black boy. I'm different. Some dudes want to be so real and care about what people think about them. They want everybody to dress like them with the big clothes that look like they're about to fly away. I have a lot of fights because of

Pernell = DOO (handwritten)

♡'s to dance (handwritten)

dance. It's just something that makes me happy. Why is everybody else worrying about it?

I grew up in the St. Bernard Housing Development, in downtown New Orleans. It's not as famous on a national level. There's been a lot of beef between people living uptown and downtown, but look how it was when we had to live in Houston after Hurricane Katrina. We all stuck together. It didn't matter what part of the city you were from—we were from New Orleans.

Daron: My sophomore year at John Mac, I enrolled in a program called the Neighborhood Story Project. At first, I just thought of it as a writing class. Most days I would come in and write raps. That was my way of expressing myself. When I didn't feel like writing, I'd fall asleep. There were just a few other students in the program and one was Pernell, who was also in Ms. Washington's second period English class with me. I remember thinking his attitude was more cocky than anything.

One day at school, I got into an argument with a group of guys I didn't really know. They wanted to jump me. Another student, D-Boi, found out what happened and asked me if I was okay. I told him, "I'm good."

But once we got out of school, the same dudes approached me again. This time, I wasn't alone. D-Boi was beside me and out of nowhere, Pernell came out saying he had my back. From that day forward, I saw he was real. He barely knew me and he had my back. I realized his cockiness was more confidence.

In English class, Pernell and I sat in the back of the class together, cracking jokes. We started hanging out at school and going to parties together.

Pernell: At first when I was in the class, I didn't know what to write about because I felt like, "If I'm going to share a story, I could just tell you."

Daron: I thought, "Man, these people all in my business. Why do they wanna know everything about me?" I thought Abram and Rachel might have been social workers trying to get in on my family business. But after I wrote a story about my uncle, I felt good. I was like, "Man, I could write more stories like this." After I read it out loud, everybody liked it, and I wanted to write more.

Pernell and I used to talk about different ways to hustle money and started saying that if we had a book, we could make money off it. I started telling him, and he used to tell me, that we needed to go to class. One day Abram and Rachel pulled Pernell and me aside and asked us if we were okay with combining our books because we had a lot in common. I found out a lot more about Pernell and his family writing this book with him.

Pernell: When I started reading Daron's work, I learned more about him as a person. We were not that different, it's just that he's from Uptown and I'm from Downtown. Then we really got serious—from writing narratives to making sure all the stories fit together. We had to get photos and interviews of our friends, family, and people who were interested in the same things we were, and had to make everything fit into one.

Daron: Writing stories, like rapping, became a way of expressing ourselves. The more I wrote, the more I realized we're losing all these people to violence. It really put a shock in our hearts. We didn't want to be the next ones in the newspaper. We didn't want to be a topic in somebody else's story.

Pernell: I'm determined to make it out.

Daron: I'm not going to say "out of the city" but I want to make a change. I don't want things to stay how they are right now because so many young people are dying every day. If you go back in John Mac over the years, the people who killed some of the students there probably went to the school, too.

Pernell: We wanted our book to talk directly to young people.

Daron: Other kids might see it and think, "Oh, they ain't been through what I've been through." Come on, man, we've lost plenty family members. We've been poor before—living in the project, mama and daddy had to sell drugs.

Pernell: Our book is about life—beyond the bricks.

The Rocheblave Court in the Calliope Projects, by Daron Crawford.

PART I: GROWING UP IN THE PROJECTS

LIVING UPTOWN AND DOWNTOWN

Daron: The Calliope's been in my blood. That's where my grandma and my mama are from, and where I grew up. My daddy's people are from Uptown off Magnolia and Amelia, but he spent so much time in the Calliope, you could say that's where he from, too. For those of you who don't know—that's in New Orleans' Third Ward—the heart of the city!

Pernell: No it isn't! [*Laughter*] Downtown by the St. Bernard Project—that's the middle of the city!

Daron: No, it's not, son! To be real, I didn't really know anything about downtown projects until after Katrina.

Pernell: In the St. Bernard, the Russells were known as the Magettes. We were always with our Grandma Maggie. There'd be 15 of us—a lot!

Daron: I went to the Bernard one time. My auntie used to live back there and I went to pick her up. We were outside and the dudes were like, "Where you from?" I said, "I'm out the Calliope." "Oh, iight." I went to playing with them.

Pernell: Nobody was gonna do you nothing. As far as I ever went uptown was the Calliope and the

Left to right: Daron's mom, Melvina, walking in the Calliope, courtesy of the Crawford family; Three girls, the Easter bunny, and house party in the St. Bernard, courtesy of the Russell family; Daron and his sister Darrion in the Calliope, courtesy of the Gordon family; and Pernell, his brother Shank, and Uncle Melvin in the St. Bernard, courtesy of the Russell family.

Melpomene Projects. I didn't feel comfortable. Like, "This not me!" Everything looked different.

Daron: I'll tell you the truth, I don't think there's a big difference. **All projects are like a village.** These are people you've been around every day.

SEGREGATION?

Daron: We didn't know too much about racism and all that at first.

Pernell: We were small! Hearing about the government separating people when they built the projects, that's stupid. It's like they didn't want people to get along. If they were living in a mixed neighborhood, they should have left it like that.

Daron: Maybe they did it like that cause the white people didn't like the black people and the black people didn't like the white people.

Pernell: But we had some white people live back there. I'd say a good 15 of them. We had this one white girl, we used to call her White Girl Glo and she had two children—they used to be outside with us, like regular people.

Daron: I don't think we had any. If they did, they never came outside or if they were white, they were black!

Pernell: Yeah!

Daron: Like, their skin was white but they had the

soul of a black person. They talked like we talk—"What's happenin, son?" It didn't seem different.

OLD AND NEW SIDES

Pernell: In the St. Bernard, we have two sides—the Old Side and the New Side. Milton splits the project in half. We stayed on the Old Side and my grandma stayed on the New. Gibson Street runs through the whole block. They called it G-Block.

Daron: I lived in the Old Side, too. We used to call ourselves the Old Side Boys.

Pernell: On the New Side, they had hallways like an apartment building.

Daron: That's how ours was, too. The New Side looked crunched up—too many people in one building.

Pernell: In my room, you could lift up the window and go sit on the fire escape.

Daron: I shared a room with my brother and sister, and then my mama and dad had a room. But then they got a futon and started sleeping downstairs, and I started sleeping in their room.

Pernell: People were always wanting to move into the project because of—

Daron: The cheap rent!

Pernell: Ours was 25 dollars. People with jobs was like 75 dollars.

WORK

Daron: A lot of people in the project worked in the hotels, cleaning up, or working in nursing homes.

Pernell: My mama sold drugs, but she also had a job. When she stopped working at the hotel on Canal Street, she went to school and got her CNA license in nursing and started going to old folks' homes and helping people. I never saw my daddy sell drugs, never. I knew he did, but I never saw him. And then he went to welding school.

Daron: A lot of people used to sell baked goods, like cakes. They had a lady who came outside when the sun went down with an ice chest full of fresh cookies. Three big old cookies for a dollar.

Pernell: We had a lady named Ms. Paula who used to sell big, fluffy cakes. When I say *good*! For my birthday, I told her to bake me a cake. One day, a dude in Parkchester, an area behind our project, shot her with a BB gun while she was riding her bike. The whole project was beating the guy up.

Daron: A lot of the old men hung out by the store.

Pernell: The old men in my court would sit under the tree and play dominoes all day.

Daron: They used to be like, "You better not do that, I'ma tell your mama."

Pernell: When we'd play football, they'd watch us.

Daron: And the younger dudes rolled dice.

SCHOOL

Pernell: My grandma was street smart—she stopped going to school in the ninth grade. My mom stopped going in the 12th grade.

Daron: I think my mama dropped out in 11th grade, but my daddy graduated from John Mac.

Pernell: My daddy graduated from Carver Senior High in the Ninth Ward.

Daron: My uncle, Derrell, dropped out in the eighth grade—he never saw high school. My cousin was the first boy to graduate. He didn't get his diploma until he was 22. He couldn't get his diploma because he didn't pass the LEAP test. He said he kept cheating. Every time he cheated off people's paper, he failed. The last time, he did it by himself, and he passed.

Pernell: Some people go to school for girls. You'll never see them in class.

Daron: Go to school to sell drugs, too. "Man, I make a killin in school, dog!"

Pernell: For real! [*Laughter*] Get their money and go home. In middle school, I used to sell games and Pokemon cards.

Daron: I used to sell candy, boy, in elementary.

Pernell: Uh huh. But for us, school was important. I liked school, boy. My mama used to check my homework and then tell me, "You straight." My daddy, he had too many rules. My dad was a real big educator.

He used to make me read chapters of books. It's Saturday—everybody's outside playing, He says, "Read three chapters of *Goosebumps* before you go outside." Boy, I didn't like all that! My daddy made me do math problems on the weekend!

Daron: My uncle used to give me money for my report card.

Pernell: Mmhm. My mama used to do that, too.

Daron: Twenty dollars for every A. Ten for every B. Five for the C's.

Pernell: D's, you didn't get nothing.

ABOUT HER BUSINESS

Daron: My mama sold drugs in Rocheblave Courtway and they had a lady who sold drugs on the other side, but my mama and her were cool so they never had problems. They had a man named T-Man. When those ecstasy pills started coming out, he decided he wanted to be the man of the project, so he knocked on the lady's door. He had a gun in his hand and said, "Don't sell no more drugs around here anymore." She had a son who'd be outside playing so she only did it on the down-low after that. For some reason, he never knocked on my mama's door.

Pernell: He didn't make her pay draft?

Daron: Nothing.

Pernell: That's what they do for scary [*afraid*] people who sell drugs in our project. They're gonna make you pay draft cause you're scary—even though you live back there! My mama acted like a dude. She didn't hang with females.

Daron: Our door got kicked in two times.

Pernell: Yeah, our door got kicked in when I was 12 years old. My mom's friend was sitting on the porch and he had crack on him, son. A police car started coming up the court and he got up, eased into our house, and locked the door. I was inside. The police kicked in the door and we ran out the back door, running through Jumonville. When I got back around, I see my mom opening the door being like, "What? What you want? What?!!" He was moving our bed and all this.

My cousin was beefing with people who'd moved in from the St. Thomas Projects. One of them shot him with a cutter [*automatic weapon*]. It went through his back and out his chest, and his arm was messed up. The police bent that arm and slammed his whole upper body on the steps. He was going crazy.

USED TO IT

Daron: One day, my mama and them were sitting on the porch, playing cards, and we heard gunshots. They didn't know which way the bullets were coming. They had a man running through the cut. Running fast. And then he went to slowing down, and dropped to the ground. Somebody ran up to him, stood over him, and emptied their clip out. Then reloaded it, emptied it again, and walked off.

Pernell: Yeah, that's why I didn't like the New Side. We were outside late playing baseball in my grandma's court and saw a big old spark from one of the porches. We ran over there and saw Marcus with blood coming out his nose. A bullet in his head. We were standing over him, looking.

Daron: The first time I had nightmares. But you know, in the project it seemed like people were getting killed every day so I was used to it. So used to it that when gunshots started to ring, we didn't run any more.

Pernell: Uh huh.

Daron: A lot of people used to run *to* the gunshots to see what's going on. One time we were standing in the courtway and we heard a car going fast-like. *Rrrrrr!* We were like, "Man! What's about to happen?" A man jumps out the car and starts shooting and somebody goes, "Pop pop pop!" from the court. He gets back in the car and by the time he gets to the end of the driveway, there's dudes with cutters in their hands, just waiting for him to come: *Drrrrrr!*

Pernell: Ak-47s. It's usually about drug dealing gone bad, somebody messing with someone's people, cliques. People used to be scared of my family, so they weren't going to tell me nothing.

Daron: They had this man named Sweet. And T-Man went to shooting at him with an AK. Sweet ran in the hallway, and T-Man was walking through the courtway with his back to him, swinging the gun. Sweet comes back out of the hallway with an L-15 and just went to spitting at him. It was like the wild, wild west. Sweet was cool, cool. He'd let us know, "Y'all get in the hallway. Go inside until they finish shootin." T-Man was that kind of man, he didn't care.

THE BEGINNING OF THE TEARDOWN

Pernell: We were still young when they started tearing down the projects in New Orleans.

Daron: We didn't really know what was going on.

Pernell: When they tore down the St. Thomas, I was thinking, "They better not tear down my hood."

Daron: When the people from St. Thomas moved into the St. Bernard, that's when a lot of problems really started in 2002. They wanted to sell their drugs, but the dudes in the St. Bernard already had their hustle. That's like trying to stop somebody's money. People aren't gonna let that happen.

Pernell: They came back there with all that stunting and bucking—they didn't come back there chillin. DJ Jubilee messed it up, son, when he started saying "St. Ber-Thomas" in his songs and then people from the St. Thomas, who moved into our project, started saying that. They were really killing people over that. They were fighting every day. I wasn't happy, but I knew it was gonna happen. And now our hoods are beefing now. Hard.

Daron: But that's not really about nothing, though. Everyone in the project isn't involved with that. It's just certain people.

Pernell: And that's why this book's important.

Daron in front of his house in the Calliope, by Susan Henry.

Daron

Roderick and Daron, courtesy of the Gordon family.

Story of My Family

My mom and dad come from two different types of families. My mom's family wasn't wealthy and had to hustle almost every dollar they had. She's the oldest of two girls and a boy and had a lot of responsibilities being that her mom wasn't home much.

My dad came from a pretty average family. He was the oldest of three and lived in a house with his mother and father. He didn't have too many responsibilities until he bumped heads with my mom when I was about three years old. My dad was only 18—very young—and didn't have any kids of his own. Here he was taking on the responsibilities of raising my sister and me, Darrion, who is only 11 months younger than me. I admit that I gave him a hard time, but not on purpose. I was young and stubborn. I talked to my parents about how we came together as a family. It felt good because it all started with Roderick just being her boyfriend and now, 16 years later, he's my dad and my best friend.

Daron: What was it like bein a single mother?

Melvina: It was hard. Your father—Count Daron—didn't want to help with Pampers, milk, or anything. He had a good mom, though. His mom used to help out.

When we lived uptown on Marengo, they stayed across the street from us. My grandmom had to go to work and my grandfather was real sick—he had cancer and was in his last stages. She asked would I stay home and take care of him. Count used to work, in his younger years, and he would come over, sit on the porch, and help me out a little bit when my grandfather would wander out of the house. But right after I had you, and then Darrion when I was 19, that was it.

Daron: How did you meet my mother?

Roderick: I met your mother at my auntie's house on Magnolia Street. I passed her on my way into the kitchen. She was sitting in the living room waiting on a ride. I told my cousin, "Look, just give her my phone number and tell her to call me." And she called me the next day. Yeah, you called me the next day.

Daron: When you started dating Dad, what was it like dating a younger man with two kids?

Melvina: Roderick and I had a lot of fun before we got married. Well, it wasn't a lot cause it was only 11 months. Eleven months of fun! [*Laughter*] We had the same needs, wants, and goals.

Roderick: We started dating—going to the casino most of the times, losing all my money. We got attached to each other and that was it.

Daron: How did y'all deal with the age difference?

Roderick: The age difference is four years. It didn't matter. You and Darrion were three and two.

Daron: Tell the story from the zoo.

Roderick: We went to McDonald's in the zoo when you were about four. You wanted a nugget meal. They didn't have any more nuggets because they were about to close. All they had were cheeseburgers. You said you didn't want the cheeseburger meal. You wanted the nuggets. I told you. "No, they don't have it." Well, you jumped up from behind me, grabbed me by my neck, choked me, and pulled me down to the floor. I could've beaten you in public, but I didn't. You were terrible. You were *very* terrible.

Melvina: He was spoiled rotten.

Roderick: Very. Darrion didn't really do anything out the ordinary but Daron was hanging around his uncle, always in the hood. You were always doing—I wouldn't say the wrong things—but doing things you just didn't have any business doing or knowing at the time.

Melvina: Like riding a go-cart at five.

Roderick: So it was a little transition. I had to shape you up—tell you, "You need to know when to be wrong and when to be right." From day one, the feelings that I had for your mom I felt for y'all. I was young myself. Basically 18.

Melvina: He lied. He was 17 and he said he was 18.

Roderick: I treated y'all as kids, but to this day I kind of treat y'all like my brother and sister rather than just being a stern parent. We kid a lot, but it's a balanced relationship where I can say, when I need to, "I'm your daddy."

friends rather than a parent

Melvina and Daron, courtesy of the Crawford family.

Daron: I'm glad you took on the responsibility, but you're crazy.

Roderick: Why? What are you doing at 18? If you had that to do at 18, you wouldn't do it?

Daron: If she had told me she had two kids I would have went on about my business and would have taken my number back.

Roderick: I basically grew up real fast. I had my own car. I used to be in a club. I used to go to the casino and just hoped they didn't ask for my ID. At that time, I had a part time job. I sold drugs then, too, but it wasn't serious. It was just tennis shoe money, gas money, insurance money. I wasn't focused on really making money because I had your mama to spend my time with. I didn't fall into that trap of I'm getting money all day, all night and I wasn't worried about no girls.

Inside the Calliope

There are two sides to the Calliope Project—Back-a-town and Front-a-town. I am from Back-a-town. There are many different courtyards and each court is different.

My court, Rocheblave, was very chilled out. There were fights every now and then, but not that much. In the Rocheblave driveway, that's where a lot of people got killed, usually over money or drugs.

One of the most dangerous courts in the project was the Thalia Court. Even though I was in that court a lot, my mom didn't like me over there. In Thalia Court, anything was likely to happen. From murders to kidnappings, to people getting stabbed up, it's all the same when it boils down. Drug dealing was the major cause of deaths in the projects, because when one person is making more money than the next person, that person would want to kill the money-maker to take their spot.

On the other side of the project was Front-a-town. It was the same as Back-a-town. It got so bad at one point that Front-a-town and Back-a-town started beefing with each other. At night time, some people from my side would go on that side and start shooting anybody they were beefing with.

The little kids used to come over to our side to fight even though we used to win. A couple of days later, we used to be right back playing with each other.

Mom: Where are you going?

Me: In Thalia.

Mom: No you are not! Are you crazy?

Me: But Mom.

Mom: But Mom nothing. You are not going over there and that is that.

Me: I'm not going to be long and I am going to be careful.

Mom: I said no and that is that.

Even though she would tell me not to go, I would just wait until she fell asleep and go over there. One day, they started shooting so my mom woke up and looked out the door to see if I was out there. When she didn't see me, she walked to Thalia looking for me. When she saw me, she grabbed me by my ears, told me to get inside, and punished me for a week.

The Candy Lady and the Sweet Shop

Ms. Dee sat outside from noon to nine at night selling her sweets. She sold anything you can name: chips, candy, cold drinks, nachos, pickles, pig lips, and much more. My favorite was the fruities. You could get 100 fruities for a dollar. I spent three dollars a day on those candies. With the money I spent, I probably could own my own fruities company by now. Once I start, I can't stop eating them.

I felt sorry for Ms. Dee because after having a good day some nights she was robbed. She was old and the police were scared to be in the project at night so there wasn't anything she could do about it. Other than that, she was doing well until the brand new and improved sweet shop opened back up in Back-a-town next to the Rite Way Store.

When the sweet shop first opened up, you used to get served out of a window in the front wall of the building. Very few people ate from there because you could never see what was going on behind that window. It wasn't making that much money and it closed down. After it closed, they started working on rehabbing the building.

At the re-opening, they gave everybody free hot dogs for a day. It seemed like the whole project was in the sweet shop. They must have given out a thousand hot dogs. They gave out so many they didn't sell any for two weeks, and when they started again, they sold out again. They were that good.

Other than good hot dogs, the new sweet shop had brand new video games, a pool table, and you finally got to see how your food was being fixed. Once the summertime came around, it started selling the best snoballs I ever tasted. Any flavor that you can name, they had it. My favorite was the wedding cake.

Even though Ms. Dee lost a lot of her customers, she was still outside every day selling her sweets. There were certain things she had that the sweet shop didn't—like those delicious fruities and those ice cold, canned, cold drinks.

Lil Derry ~ uncle-drug dealer

My uncle, Lil Derry, is short, and used have dreads in his head until he went to jail and they made him cut them off.

In the mornings, on our way to catch the bus, he used to pick us up, bring us to McDonald's, and then bring us to school. Some days he would try and help us with our homework, even though he didn't know how to do it. He used to tell us to stay away from selling drugs. That it's not the right way to get your money. There's a quote he used to use, "Fast money is not the right money."

He was a drug dealer for a living. He dealt in the Third Ward on Louisiana and Loyola. Sometimes I would try to hang out with him, but he didn't like me around the dealing. He told me he had started around the age of 12. His mom was on drugs and his dad was in prison. My mom had to take care of him and their two other sisters. She did the best she could until their grandmother started helping out.

Some days we could hear his car from six blocks away because the bumping music was so loud. We would run downstairs, and he would already be out there screaming our names. When we made it down there, he would pop his trunk and have a whole bunch of shoeboxes. We would find our size, give him a hug, tell him thank you, and try them on.

Interview with My Mother, Melvina Crawford

My mom's a happy person. In the morning time, she wakes up with a smile. When I'm upset, she tells me she loves me and I got to get it together. I've seen her do the same for years. We could be going through hard times but she still stays focused. Through her, I'm learning how to be a good parent for when I have kids. The interview was emotional. You could hear pain in her voice, but she still was able to laugh at some of the craziness. She's also a great storyteller. One story I used to hear her tell a lot was when a bully kept messing with her, and finally, her mama told her that she had to fight the girl. She didn't want to do it, but she knew if she didn't handle the situation, it wasn't going to stop. I've always thought that story was a good metaphor for how my mom moves through the world. She doesn't like conflict, but she handles her business.

Melvina, by Daron Crawford.

Daron: Where were you born and raised?

Melvina: In New Orleans, Louisiana, in the Calliope Housing Development.

Daron: Where did our family live before the Calliope?

Melvina: In the Uptown area of Marengo and Freret.

Daron: Do you know very much about the family history?

Melvina: No, sad to say.

Daron: Who did you grow up with?

Melvina: My grandma, my uncle and auntie. My mom wasn't too much around. She was on drugs and she was homeless, so we stayed with my grandmom.

Daron: How was your relationship with your grandmother?

Melvina: Real good. [*Laughter*] Her name was Wilhelmina Broomfield, a sweet old lady. She was real happy, no matter what.

Daron: What are some of the things that y'all did together, talked about?

great grandmother [handwritten annotation with arrow pointing to "grandmother"]

19

Melvina: I used to have a lot of questions about why my mom was acting the way she was and not coming home. She was like, "Just put it in God hands and pray for her." She used to always say, "She's sick." I couldn't understand it. She had all these kids and she'd rather be somewhere else knowing that we didn't have anybody in the home to teach us right from wrong or help my sisters and my brother. We would always have to wait til the weekend and go by grandmom and ask these questions. We got better answers from grandma.

We had a step-dad. He was a good step-dad—that's my brother Derry and my sister's dad. He was a good role model in the home, and I guess that's why I got a lot of wanting more—pushing for the education. Then he tried to travel with her to bring her back from drugs, and he got caught up.

He would bring money into the home. She'd say I stole it. She'd take clothes, shoes out of the home, have my younger sisters and brother looking for them. I didn't know how to tell them that she had stolen them to sell them. I remember my step-dad argued with her about spending too much money, and she acted as if she was spending it on us, which sometimes she did. But like I said, when night falls, you go to look for those things and they're gone.

My mom wasn't the only one of her siblings on drugs. That's why my grandmom had to hide a little money and jewelry. Still, she would try to sneak and give them 20 dollars from her husband. He was mean. He was like, "Oh, here come the people from the bricks." He called the projects the bricks. "Hide the pots!" He would actually go run inside and try to put up the pots. He didn't want to do anything for anybody, but

Melvina's mother, courtesy of the Crawford family.

my grandmom's heart wouldn't allow that. If he was sitting on the front porch and she had to sneak to the side door and give you something to eat, that's just what it was gonna be.

He was one of those cat daddies. He had this long gray hair and my grandma would perm it and roll it up on Fridays. He would leave on Friday with all the jewelry on and come back on Sunday. And my grandmom accepted it. I guess that was her breathing time and her free time. She was like, "I'm gonna roll his hair and do whatever he needs me to do."

Daron: What did she do for a living?

Melvina: My grandma worked in Ye Olde College Inn. It used to be a nice little restaurant on Carrollton Avenue. She was a cook there for something like 28 years. In the morning, she would have a cold Coke before work. She wore the little white uniform. When she got off, she kept her little dress on and walked around with her Daniel Green slippers. In the evening, she had a beer.

At the College Inn, she had like a tab to where she could get meat during the week and they would take it out of her check on a Friday. She was able to get a little smoke sausage, pork chops, and she'd make large pots to stretch it. She'd never refuse anyone food.

I remember one time we had green peas and smoke sausage [*Laughter*]. Uncle Willie was my rowdiest uncle—him and my mom used to always get into it, and they were running my grandmother's pressure up. I was in the kitchen holding you, and my uncle Henry Smith, aka Peanut—he owns his own home in Houston right now. He moved off from the family and he's doing real good—got so mad that they were making my grandma sick, he's like, "Y'all gonna kill my mama!" He smacked the pot of green peas, and it went all over you, Daron. You were just crying and I went to crying. He smacked those green beans on my baby.

Daron: How was your relationship with your mother?

Melvina: It was shaky with the drugs and all, and I had to take on a lot of responsibilities with raising my sisters and my brother.

Daron: How was your relationship with your father?

Melvina: It was phone calls, a visit here and there. Distant.

Daron: Do you wish that you saw him or talked to him more?

Melvina: I guess by me being a girl, I wished my mom was around more. I really needed her, you

Henry Smith, aka Uncle Peanut, courtesy of the Brumfield family.

know. But I love my dad—my dad and I have a strong relationship now. He's in Houston, but we talk. Me and my mom as well, but we can't be together too long. [*Laughter*] One day out of the week, I go by her house, do her hair, talk to her a little. She tells me now that she appreciated me being there for my sisters and my brother. Every time we'll have problems, she'll remind them that I was there for them.

DRUGS

Daron: Did you enjoy your days in the Calliope Projects?

Melvina: I guess in my younger days, but not as I got older. We moved into the Calliope when I was ten years old after living with my grandmother. In those years, we stayed by Booker T. Washington Senior High on Erato Street, and I was on my mom's lease. When I made 18, I was able to get a unit of my own. And I stayed in a unit on Earhart with my two kids, Daron and Darrion.

Daron: Why not?

Melvina: When I was younger, I didn't really understand or want more, so it was just all about play. But as you got older, you see a lot of crime and no future for your kids, so it makes you want to get away.

Daron: And by more you mean?

Melvina: Better living, education.

Daron: How old were you when you started selling drugs?

Melvina: Maybe about 16. We moved out of B.W. Cooper—something to do with my mom wasn't paying a bill, and I took my sisters and my brother and moved uptown by Walter L. Cohen on Delachaise Street. It was real hard. It was just me and them, and I started selling marijuana.

Daron: Who taught you how to sell drugs?

Melvina: [*Laughter*] I would say that had to be my little brother.

Daron: What was my uncle Lil Derry like when he was growing up?

Melvina: He loved football. He's fast—very fast. [*Laughter*] He's real small to be 30. He played the trumpet and he also played the snare drum. He chipped his teeth one time on the snare drum. He was his daddy's baby.

Daron: When he was younger did you see any stages that stood out?

Melvina: Yeah, he was a real happy child. He had to be somewhere around 13 when he started trying to sell drugs.

Top: Tasha, Lil Derry, and Melvina. *Bottom:* Shanel and Darrion. Photograph courtesy of the Crawford family.

Daron: And who taught him how?

Melvina: He sat back real quiet and watched my mom go out spending the money that she was supposed to be spending on us. He's a fast learner, so he caught on real quick that crack was selling. Seeing my mom and them do the drugs, it's just like he didn't want no more. He dropped out of school in seventh or eighth grade. He really wanted my mom off drugs.

Daron: When did you notice that change in him from him being this happy child to being a person on the streets?

Melvina: One time, he had some drugs from some guy, and my mom took the drugs and smoked them. My brother didn't have no other way to give this person their money so they got into it, and it seemed like from there on out, he was just in the streets.

Daron: And how did you feel about him selling drugs?

Melvina: I felt like he was too young, but at the same time, kids rib a lot: "Look at your shoes." "Look at your clothes." He wasn't one of those people that just sat around and took it. He always was a go–getter. I mean, that was the wrong way to do it, but—

Daron: So would you say it was peer pressure from the kids?

Melvina: I would say it was just wanting and needing. My mom would even take the food stamps that the government was giving us and she would sell that.

Daron: How old was Derry the first time he went to jail?

Melvina: I'm gonna say 16. He had purchased his own car, a nice little Cutlass. He got stopped and went to jail for possession of crack cocaine. From 16 to 20, he went to jail maybe three times. Whenever he was about to be arrested, he would always run and got "resisting arrest" on top of the other charges.

When he made 19, he was facing five years. My mom got control on her habit as she saw he was really starting to be out there. She used to go down to the courthouse and do a lot of work for judges—cleaning up their houses—and she started knowing a good bit of people down there. She talked to the judge and instead of the five years, he sent Derry to a halfway house for two years.

Daron: Did that have a big effect on the family?

Melvina: Yeah. Everybody wanted to find a way to get money to give to him because he was the only boy. Nobody wanted to see him in the streets like that, but it wasn't enough cause he had gotten used to a large amount.

REAL LIVING

Daron: How did you feel about moving from New Orleans when I was little?

Melvina: To Vegas? It made my stomach swirl as if you're in a courthouse. It was the first time I ever got on a plane. We had one-way tickets. All these thoughts started wandering about, "Maybe we might get to Vegas and he might leave me," but I just put it in God's hands.

His aunt was saying, "This is gonna be good. Y'all are gonna have a job like the day after you get here." When we got there, she said, "You're gonna have your own room at my house." We got there to find that she was on drugs, she had these big old dogs in the house, and I was frightened of dogs.

The following day, we tried to see what the county was offering for assistance, and they gave us welfare and food stamps. We found an apartment *way* on the other side of town. Roderick went to work, cause that's Roderick—he's a real man. I was still homesick—throwing up, just balling up. Me and you rode the East Tropicana bus from one part of Vegas to the other side and moved three large duffle bags. We stayed in that empty apartment no more than a month. We had a little TV, bed. Everybody was real happy, real happy.

23

Daron: Did you have any culture shocks, or were there a lot of changes from New Orleans to Las Vegas?

Melvina: I think I matured a lot when we went to Vegas cause that was real living. In Vegas, it's like the sky is the limit, and it felt real good just trying to touch it. Roderick went to Dillard's and he sold men's shoes. He got a nice commission check, and we were able to pay the lights and the rent. And then I had got a nice job at Palace Station Casino doing housekeeping, which was unionized—the pay started off with $10.00 a hour, when something in New Orleans started you out at $6.00 an hour.

Daron: How did it feel being away from home when your grandmother passed?

Melvina: That was hard. We didn't have the money for me to come back to New Orleans. I had just got pregnant with little Roderick. By the time I got here, they had already buried my grandmom, so I wasn't able to see her. But I have this picture of her that I will never forget—as I can remember, my grandmom was a real strong lady.

Daron: Did anything special happen while you were in Las Vegas?

Melvina: Yeah, Lil Roderick was born. [*Laughter*] I was doing housekeeping and I used to smile a lot. One of the housekeepers came to get me for lunch one day, and she was just standing up there looking, and I never turned around—I was just smiling, cleaning

Melvina, Daron, Darrion, and Roderick in Las Vegas, courtesy of the Gordon family.

up. She say, "Mel, you like cleaning those toilets?" [*Laughter*] I was just so happy, and I remember just smiling so hard my cheekbones used to hurt.

Daron: Oh, man, wow.

Melvina: I had a wonderful husband, and wonderful children. You were a real responsible child. One time when you were about seven, you came home from school and the lights were off. You took your basketball and went to the basketball court. We came home from work—the lights were off, no Daron. Roderick said, "Let's go walk to the basketball court." There you were, like you didn't have a worry in the world.

Daron: What was it like, you know, moving back to the projects after being away?

Melvina: That was the worst thing I ever did in my whole life. I guess the homesickness never really went away. I was pregnant and my mom, my sisters, and a friend of theirs came out to visit. They stayed there about four days, and they stayed in the house with us. And then we had to bring them to the airport, and watching them leave, it was like they had taken something away.

After we had Lil Roderick, I wanted to go home. Roderick used to always tell me, "If we stay here, we almost there. You can get you a truck." You know, "We can do this, we can that." I wanted it, but I wanted to be back with my family.

Daron: Have you ever got caught selling drugs?

Melvina: Yes, I did. At 23 years old, my door was kicked in. I was in the Calliope and I was selling crack cocaine.

Daron: What were the consequences?

Melvina: I went to jail. I spent seven days in jail and I had $120,000 bond. My husband went to jail, cause when the door got kicked in, he went as well. His bond was $100,000. But his family is a little fortunate, so they were able to get him out. I think he only spent three or four days—then he had to get the money to get me out. It's something like ten percent.

We weren't doing any major drug selling. It was just knocks at the door. By the time you go and spend money to purchase it and then you break it down to sell it and you take shorts, you barely have enough to go and re-up.

Daron: Do you think it had an effect on your family's life?

Melvina: I may be wrong, but we kept nothing from our kids. We kept it open so that they could see what was going on. It makes it easier to explain to y'all, you know, that the things we had then, we don't have them now. But we don't have to be looking over our shoulders. It's better living, you know. I think seeing your parents go through that made y'all a little stronger and wiser.

Daron: Like the fact that you all were cutting it in front of us, we knew that it wasn't the right thing, but that was what y'all needed to do to help the family out and times were hard. I mean, I couldn't ask for, you know, a better parent than I have.

Melvina: And I love you for that. [*Laughter*]

Daron: I love you more.

Darrion, Melvina, Lil Roderick, Roderick, and Daron, courtesy of the Gordon family.

Growing up with Drugs

Growing up in a house where drugs were sold wasn't as bad as you think it would be. Don't get me wrong, there have been some nights where I wasn't able to go to sleep comfortably because I was scared, but my dad made me feel protected. My dad had two guns in the house. He always kept the guns in safe places to prevent accidents, but he always told me that he wouldn't let anything bad happen to our family.

My dad would stay up all night and all day, but he never got tired. I don't know how he did it, but I guess the dollar signs kept him up. Friday night was our family night. We all would sit in the living room, pop popcorn, and crack jokes with each other.

We never could watch a whole movie without pausing at least ten times because of the knocks on the door. My brother, my sister, and I never got mad because we know that they were selling drugs to support us.

On September 4, 2004, my dad was helping me out with my homework and my mother was cooking. Out of nowhere we heard two big bangs going against our back door. The cops rushed in with their big guns and bright flashlights, demanding everyone to get on the floor.

They handcuffed my mom and dad and sat them on the bed. My brother and sister were very scared. I was scared also.

They ripped the house up from upstairs to downstairs, looking for drugs. They were getting very mad because they couldn't find anything. They brought their K9 into the house. The dog looked very vicious. My brother started screaming his lungs out once the dog got close to him. My mom did a good job calming him down, saying that it was going to be all right.

Cops didn't find anything. They took my brother, sister, and me into another room, telling us to tell them where the drugs were at and saying how they are trying to help us. All we were saying was, "We don't know what you are talking about." And we stuck to our words.

They finally uncuffed my mom and dad and told them that they were going to be back so they'd better watch themselves.

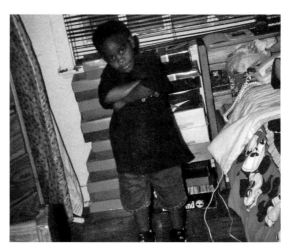

Daron with his shoe boxes in the Calliope, courtesy of the Crawford family.

Showing Love

I wouldn't say that my dad had a lot of haters because he showed love and when you show love in the projects, you get love back.

Every now and then we would hear about somebody saying they wanted to rob him, but nobody ever grew the balls to try him—he was too respected. My dad helped out a lot of people in the projects when they were doing badly. There was this man that lived around the driveways from us named Terryon. Terryon fixed on our cars and when he didn't have any money and needed to feed his kids, my dad would give him 20 dollars.

When we used to go on vacation out of town, my dad would give Terryon 30 dollars to watch the house for us.

Sometimes when the drug users didn't have money, my dad would let them hold something until they got paid, and the users would tell my dad if they heard anything about the police planning to come through.

Interview with My Dad, Roderick Gordon

I really wanted to interview my dad because I wanted to know how he felt staying up all those nights in the Calliope serving customers. I knew a good bit of them and despite the stereotypes about "crack heads" a lot of them acted normal. They had money, too. They came from other parts of the project and my dad treated them like friends. Sometimes, if they didn't have the money, he let them barter. Say if I had a flat on my bike, my dad would let one of them change it in exchange for a fix. He always told me as long as somebody respect you, treat them the same.

I also wanted to talk to my dad about why we decided to move back to New Orleans from Las Vegas, and what it was like to come back to the Calliope. My dad grew up around the Magnolia and the Calliope and had seen the rise of Cash Money and No Limit Records. He saw how project boys could become so big. Even though, in some ways, my parents saw coming back to the Calliope as a step down, music from the projects of New Orleans could be seen as a way to move back up.

Daron: This is Daron Crawford and I'm interviewing Chevy Earnhard. Where were you born and raised?

Roderick: I was born and raised in New Orleans, Louisiana. I spent half of my life downtown in the Seventh Ward, and after my mom and dad's divorce, we moved uptown. I left due to the circumstances at home and lived with my auntie on Magnolia Street, a block away from the Magnolia Project. That's where I spent my life up until I met my wife, and then I lived in the Calliope Project.

Daron: Can you tell me about your parents?

Roderick, by Abram Himelstein.

Roderick: My dad didn't graduate from high school, but he got a GED and did a little time in college, but it wasn't for him. The only good paying job that he was able to find was with the Merchant Marines, which meant he was gone for eight months of the year. It put a real strain on the relationship cause he wasn't home and, you know, women have wants and needs. So it got pretty bad.

Daron: Can you name something in your life that you did that wasn't right but you just had to do it?

Roderick: The one thing I did that wasn't right was selling drugs. At the time, I thought that I had to do it, but realistically nobody has to do things of that nature that they know they shouldn't be doing.

When we came back from Vegas, I began to sell drugs real hard. It was a corner I forced myself into because I had the choice not to leave Vegas. I knew. I grew up here, and I made that conscious choice for family and friends and just the love of this city to come back.

To be honest with you, Las Vegas was a party city, too, but it was still different. They didn't have second lines on Sundays or DJs in the street. Everything was real fast out there. It was either gambling, or you on your way to or from work. There was nobody in the backyard with a barbecue grill. The family aspect was missing. We used to go to parks to do picnics and we missed the oak trees. We missed walking between the streetcar tracks on the neutral ground just talking. You really begin to understand the culture of New Orleans and what you're missing once you leave it.

Daron: Do you regret going?

Roderick: I don't regret going at all because it opened my eyes to a different lifestyle. I worked, I clocked in on somebody's clock, I paid bills, I got a real respect for the responsible world. Before that, we were living in the housing development. Rent was $34.00. We didn't have a light bill to pay, it didn't make you want to go out and find a job, because, "Hey, I'm living for free. I could hustle some money, It'll be all right."

Daron: What did you learn from hustling in the projects?

Roderick: The management experience we learned in the drug trade went into the music business that came out of the projects.

Daron and Darrion dancing in Las Vegas, courtesy of the Gordon family.

Cash Money was from the Magnolia and Master P was from the Calliope. He and his brothers developed a lot of different groups and solo artists. I have a lot of respect and admiration for those type of cats. Juvenile—you would catch him on Louisiana Avenue by the store Keys—just parked out there with the door bust open, music blaring.

A lot of the artists from down here, they're pretty humble. For the most part, they go where they go by themselves—no security, no police. They walk the streets like men. I have a lot of respect for those guys that paved the way—just showing us you could be what you want. You could do what you want. Don't let nobody stop you.

Songs I Listened to

When I was young, No Limit Records was just taking over the national airwaves, and everyone in the project was happy for them. They used to come back and show love with summer camps and putting us in their videos. I went to two of their basketball summer camps and they used to come play and talk with us about staying focused in school. They told us we could make it just like them if we put our mind to it. The stay in school message stuck to us just as much as their music.

Around 1998, Cash Money from Uptown started to blow up, too, and my family was close to a lot of the members. My auntie Tasha used to conversate with Turk, one of the members of the original Hot Boyz. When he came by our house in the Calliope, he seemed very cool and quiet, which I didn't get from him in his videos where he acted wild and hyped, jumping all over the camera.

My mama was very cool with B.G. Sometimes she would pick me from my grandma's house on Amelia Street and B.G. would be in the car with his headphones on, beating on the backseat, rapping.

When his song "Bling, Bling" came out, my brother and I used to put on these gold chains with our initials on them that our parents bought us for Christmas, and perform the song in front of the T.V. My favorite lines were:

"You could see my neck from a mile, Bling Bling!"

At the time, the other rappers that were big in the projects were Soulja Slim and VL Mike who were full on gangsta rappers. But to clear my mind, I listened to more national rappers like T.I. and Jay-Z. Their songs, I felt, were about my life. T.I.'s "24's" is an example of what I wanted from life back then: nice cars and big rims, and Jay-Z's "Hard Knock Life" was important because I felt like living in a project and overcoming it would be a great battle.

After a few summers of the Master P summer camp, I decided to play basketball for the New Orleans Recreation Department. Most of the guys were from the Calliope. I kept my CD player on repeat before a game, playing Master P's "Bout It, Bout It" to get myself hyped. The song's beat would be banging:

"I represent where the killas at
Third Ward, Back-a-town
Calliope, we on the map."

Rapping

I was sitting in the living room with my dad playing Madden on PlayStation 2. All of a sudden, there was a knock at the door—a knock that would eventually change my whole life.

It was my dad's brother, Craig. He came in with a CD and told us to put it on. It was a CD with him rapping on it. It sounded like he took pride in his lyrics. He had a laid back, can't-touch-me style and he wasn't spitting the same tired cliches.

It sounded like talent. My dad really liked it. He had written in the past and knew how much work went into making a good song. My dad told Craig that he would pay for the studio time, but he had to be serious about it. They started a group called Street Team.

Every time they went to Festival Studio across the river, I came, too, and really started to get interested in it. I used to go into the mirror and just play around, putting on my Fitty hat backwards with my gold chain around my neck and try to rap to myself. One day, we were in the living room. He was writing to a beat and I was playing Grand Theft Auto. I threw down the joystick and said, "Man, I'm tired of this. I want to rap."

He paused the music and laughed at me, then asked if I was serious.

I said, "I'm for real! I really want to rap."

"All right. Get a pen and some paper and I'm gonna help you with your first one." The lyrics were an intro to my new career:

Even though I'm too young to get in the club
I slide in unnoticed cause I'm rollin with thugs.
It's Street Money, baby. Yeah, we're official
Authentic street figures like a ref with a whistle.

He brought me to the studio to do the song. I was nervous and couldn't stay on beat. It took me at least an hour to get the rap down pat. When I heard myself on the song after it was finished, it made me want to do more and more songs.

One day Craig, my daddy, and I were sitting on the porch and Craig told my dad that he gave his mixtape to one of Lil Wayne's artists. My dad told him that he had to watch who he hands his music out to. For no reason, Craig went to going off, "Don't fucking tell me what to do!"

My daddy was taken aback, "Who you talking to?"

"I'm fuckin talkin to you!"

"Lil boy, you better calm down." My daddy stood up. Craig got in his face and said, 'I'ma pop your fuckin chain."

My dad walked off. That was the end of Street Team.

I'm On

My dad stopped worrying about rap and started his Gordon & Sons Mobile Detailing Service. I was still writing in my free time, not letting my dad know.

At Valence C. Jones in the Seventh Ward, we used to beat on the lunch table and rap every day, surrounded by a crowd of other students. It was five of us: T-Mike, Kenyon, De'Juan, and Lil E were out of the Seventh Ward. I was the only one from Uptown. We called ourselves D-Block after the rap group from New York with Jadakiss. T-Mike was the best rapper of us all. What can I say, the kid had talent. Kenyon could hit all of the cold beats without missing a note. Lil E was the hype man. He drew a lot of attention to us. I was the second best rapper. De'Juan was not as dedicated, he just knew how to rap, so he wasn't as cold as T-Mike and me.

One day we were rapping at the lunch table and the four dudes from the classroom next door called us out. They said, "Give us ten minutes and I bet we can make a better song than y'all." We said, "Okay."

The four guys from next door came out with their rap first and had the lunchroom rocking like a rock concert. We didn't even know what we were going to do. All I heard was T-Mike telling Kenyon to drop the beat. Once Kenyon started beating on the table, T-Mike came in with his verse saying, "15 years on this earth, I done did my dirt," and following it up with the things he had done wrong, how he smoked weed and toted guns. So as T-Mike finished, I hopped in, starting my verse just like his, finishing up with the things I have done wrong in my life. I told people how I pooed my Pampers and peed on whoever tried to change my diapers. Now that was bad. De'Juan was the last to go. He started his verse off just like us, but finished it up saying things he didn't want to have to go through. The lunchroom went crazy over his ending. We won and held onto our title all the way until we graduated from middle school.

T-Shirts

Ever since I can remember, t-shirts were made for celebrations. Every time somebody had a birthday party they got t-shirts made— not just for the person whose birthday it was, but everybody who was coming to the party. They also were bought when it was time for a family member to graduate. There wasn't one event that went by that people didn't get t-shirts made. And, of course, there were those sad times when people died, so family members got R.I.P. shirts. Those are probably the most selling t-shirts, even though that's sad to say. Some of the shirts would say "Sunrise" and there would be the person's date of birth and the other side would say, "Sunset" which would have the date that the person died. Others said "Thugged in" and "Thugged out."

I'm Sagging Now

I was inside watching reruns and out of nowhere I heard my uncle's loud music bumping four blocks away. I ran down the stairs. He pulled in front of the door and I told him how bored I was. He said, "Come with me. I'm bout to go to the mall." I jumped in his green two-door Tahoe, and we pulled off. He was blaring State Property so loud it felt like my ear drums were going to pop.

We went to the mall tucked around by the Supe rdome. The first place we went was Foot Locker. He bought us both Nikes. Then we went to the hip hop clothes store. My uncle told me to get a pair of jeans to try on so I grabbed the Rocawear jeans that I had been wanting with the big "R" on them. I went into the dressing room and put them on. I was looking in the mirror like, "Yeah, this me," and came out to let my uncle see.

He said, "Boy, you better go take them tight ass jeans off." They weren't really tight—just weren't baggy. He threw me a pair that were two sizes bigger than I needed. Thoughts were running through my mind about what my mama was going to say and all I heard in the back of my mind was, "Pull them God-damn pants up." But I still let him buy them for me.

When I got home, my mama told me to try them on so she could see what they looked like. When I came down, I walked kind of slow so I wouldn't trip over the pants and fall down the stairs. She didn't say anything, just shook her head like she wanted to grab me by my pants and whip my ass. But she didn't— she let it slide.

My uncle took me to a concert that night. I looked and felt like a gangsta and all the ladies were looking. I had so much fun that night but to be honest I don't like my jeans that big. I'm not gonna say I never bought another big pair of jeans, but I don't wear them too often.

The Good Old Days

My lil dog Darnell and I had been friends for years. When I showed up with my baggy jeans, he said, "You done switched yo style up, huh?"

I felt like a new person and said, "You see me, huh?" He'd seen me go through a bunch of stages in my life, and we knew everything about each other. He lived with his grandmother because his dad was locked up and his mom lived out of town.

We met each other when I was about eight. We were both went to the Youth Educational Town, which was an after school program for the youth located in the back of the projects. They had a big kid by the name of Corey who picked on everybody. One day, I came outside in the yard and saw Corey pushing on Darnell. I said, "Let him go."

Corey said, "Who is you?"

"I'm Daron."

"What if I push on you?"

I admit I was scared, but I said, "And I would fuck you up." He left Darnell alone and walked up to me and pushed me down. I fell so hard, I didn't want to get back up, but all of the girls were watching. I stood up and gave him one hard punch to the face and he backed up out of the fight. I felt like I was the man. Darnell, on the other hand, was kind of mad cause he had needed the help.

He came up to me and asked me my name and shook my hand. And from that day on, if somebody was looking for me, just find Darnell and vice versa. Whatever I did, he did. Playing basketball, football, and rapping. Darnell couldn't rap that good, but I could never beat him in basketball cause he was so quick on his feet. But when I was outside the three point line, no one could stop me. If you try to jump and block my shot, you'd be mad, cause I make them more than the Army shoots bullets.

"You Scary"

When someone says that, you know the peer pressure has begun. It's one of the biggest blames for why young black boys are robbing, beating people up, or killing. But if you are one of the kids who goes to school and does what you have to do, that doesn't make you uncool. Everyone knows the outcomes of succumbing. There is a saying, "When they end up dead or in jail, you will have a nice paying job."

Like this one time. All the homies were sitting on the porch. One dude came out with a fake gun and said, "Let's go rob the corner store." One of the guys said, "D, here's the gun. You go in there first and I'm gone come in behind you." At first I thought they were playing, but come to find out this wasn't the first time they did something like this. Once I saw there were serious, I said, "Man, I ain't doing it."

They said, "You fucking scary."

I said, "Bitch, I ain't scary. I'm just not stupid."

"Man, fuck you."

By me being the person I am, I said, "Let's fight."

We both got off the porch and as soon as we threw our hands up, the police came through the cut. They told everybody to put our hands on the porch. They found the gun on my lil partner who had been holding it, but after they realized it was a fake, they brought him to his mom and he got punished for a month.

As far as them other lil dudes, they didn't even exist to me anymore. A couple of weeks later, they tried to carry out the robbery with a real gun and the police caught them in the act.

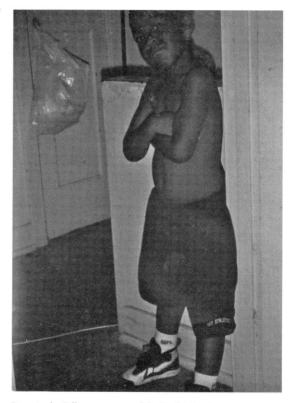

Daron in the Calliope, courtesy of the Gordon family.

Mistaken Identity

uncle=Derry

In 2004, my uncle Derry and friends came to my house and we played "NBA in the Street" for ten dollars a game. One of the friends kept saying, "We need a truck." Lil Derry said, "Don't worry bout it." They got up and started walking out the door. My mama said, "Lil Derry, don't go do nothin stupid."

The same night, we got a call saying he was in jail.

It was a short conversation and we didn't know what happened until we went to pay his bond. He came back to our house and told us the story.

That night he got dropped off at his usual set on Louisiana and Loyola. When his friend came back, he was driving a truck with an illegal loaded weapon. When they got to a red light, the cops turned on their sirens. The dude and my uncle jumped out of the truck and the gun fell out of the dude's lap. My uncle looked just like the dude, so the cops couldn't tell the difference and brought them both to Orleans Parish Prison.

They both had to talk to the cops. His friend walked to the cell that my uncle was in and said, "Yes, that's him. He stole the car and had the gun in his lap," and it was all over for my uncle. He was sentenced to eight years, mandatory five.

My uncle is the D in my dog.
And to all my haters, forget them all.

We used to wild out at the mall.
Now I sit in my room waiting on that collect call.

For all those who stayed loyal, I respect y'all.
And to the haters, you better wear your vest, dog.

Cause the tool a leave a couple of nails in your chest, dog.
I leave your head on your body and take the rest off.

My clique is real so don't test mine.
I say four words, "Who's next in line?"

And to those bragging, saying they get the cake.
Deep inside they really fake.

They ain't popping no guns
All they doing is popping off by the gums.

I'm going to be on top, ain't no maybe.
Even though I'm real, the game is shady.

Dark Clouds

The last few days before Katrina felt so normal. Friday after school, I played football in my court until the streetlights came on. Then everybody sat on the porch and ate icebergs. Only one thing seemed different—the mean old lady who lived near us sat on the porch and laughed while we cracked jokes. Usually if we made too much noise, she called the police.

After dark, we decided to play Nigga Knock. In the project that's this game where you ring somebody's doorbell and run when you hear them coming. We felt so free running through the project, looking back at all of the people sitting on the porch with their beers on a Friday night after a long week of work. When I got inside the food on the stove was cold and the family was asleep.

I was sure I'd wake up to gunshots but this Saturday there were no gunshots heard at all. My mom fixed a big breakfast for us—pancakes, grits, and eggs. Afterwards, we sat in the living room watching the news. We got a call from my uncle Peanut saying that we should leave for the storm. My dad agreed and called it our vacation.

Dark clouds covered the sun and the buildings of the project. After packing my clothes, I stood on my top porch asking all of my friends if they were leaving. I saw Darnell and told him we were going to Houston. Darnell said, "Well, okay, I'm gonna holla at you when you get back." We dapped each other off—the last dap we have had.

Rocheblave Court, by Daron Crawford.

Pernell at his dad's house, by Abram Himelstein.

Pernell

Story of My Family

My mama and my daddy come from big families— my mama with eight brothers and sisters and my daddy with 14. My mama is from the St. Bernard Public Housing Development and my daddy is from the Desire Public Housing Development in the Ninth Ward. They started talking on the phone when she was 13 and he was 15.

Four years later, my daddy moved in with my mother at my grandmother's house in the St. Bernard, and she got pregnant with me. My mama was a senior at John McDonogh Senior High and she had to drop out. My daddy went to welding school and started working at Bollinger's Shipyard.

I was born small and almost died. I was five pounds, five ounces.

When I was about one, my mama and daddy moved into the house I was raised: 1325 Foy, the realest court in the St. Bernard. I went to a nursery called New Day that was in my court right by the sprinklers. My parents would be at work so after school, so I used to go by my grandmother's house with my aunties. My daddy worked in the morning and got off at night and my mother worked at night until wee hours. Sometimes my mama would be home and her boss would call her. She would leave me inside with snacks and the phone on the bed. I would watch T.V. until my daddy came home. I remember calling my mama crying because I was scared inside by myself.

Pernell as a baby, courtesy of the Russell family.

She asked, "You crying?" And I said, "No."

I started to live with my grandmother Maggie. She had seven kids at the time, so I was never alone. My grandma was known for being a loudmouth in the projects. She could be on one end and call some one on the other side. I remember times when my Maw-maw would come get me late at night, and the police would stop us because she was so small—about four feet eight inches tall. Then they would get close and see that she was older, and she would say, "What dick sucking bitches."

But the thing I remember most is that my grandmother was a kindhearted person. She brought people up to me and say, "This is my grandson." I would tell her to stop showing me to people and she would say, "You ain't all that."

An Effect On Me

When I was about four, my daddy went to jail and told my mom to go on with her life. She started talking to Boo. He's how my brother Kelin—who we call Shank—came along. *brother*

When my daddy got out, I was six. He was upstairs asleep and Boo came by our house and started fighting with my mama. My daddy must have heard and came downstairs and started to beat Boo up. As he walked out the door he yelled, "Y'all started a war." I ran to the door and said, "Boo, where you going?" She told me, "Get your ass back in here." *other brother*

When I was eight, Rasheed was born. I was mad because there were less toys for me. Yes, I'm selfish. I don't care. My little brother grew up fast and soon I didn't care about toys. I started talking to girls on the phone and moved over to Edward Henry Phillips Junior High—my favorite school. My dad and my mama broke up. It had a little effect on me.

Pernell Senior with Kelin, Pernell, and Melvin, courtesy of the Russell family.

Interview with My Mom, Latica Russell

My mama is this little black lady with burgundy hair and two golds in her mouth.

She is my friend, my homie, my everything. I can go to her and tell her anything. She tries to tell me right from wrong, but always lets me choose my own way.

My mama really likes children. I remember during the holidays in the project, if someone didn't have anything, she would buy it for them. Then I would tell her, "Ma, you doing that for them, but would they do it for us?" She'd always say, "Don't be like that, bae."

I wanted to interview my mama because I knew she had a lot to talk about. She always tells me stories about back in the day when she was growing up. I was happy for her to share some of them with everyone.

Pernell: So where did you grow up?

Tica: In the St. Bernard Housing Development.

Pernell: What did your mother do for a living?

Tica: My mama worked at the shrimp factory. She worked at a hotel. She worked at McDonald's. She worked at another restaurant—Steak and Eggs. She had a lot of jobs.

Pernell: What did your father do?

Tica: He worked on houses.

Pernell: How did you feel when they split up?

Pernell and Latica, by Abram Himelstein.

Tica: Mmm. It wasn't the same when they split up. It wasn't the same. My mama was 14 when she got pregnant with me.

Pernell: How old my grandpa was?

Tica: My daddy was in his early 20s.

Pernell: And she was 14?!

Tica: Once my daddy and my mama split up, they didn't get back together, so it was just the two of us in the household. I ain't really had no hard, rough life cause my mama worked, even though she had got on drugs right after that. She dressed me in clothes from the department stores on Canal Street—D.H. Holmes, Krauss. I wore the best. I better not get off the porch and go play with the little children until she changed my clothes. Their mama doesn't work and spend all their money on them like my mama used to do with me.

My daddy was from Violet in the St. Bernard Parish, but he came through every holiday to give my sister and me our allowance. He called us Chocolate and Vanilla cause she's red and I'm dark.

Tica and her mother, Maggie Russell, courtesy of the Russell family.

When I was about six, I asked my daddy for a dog. He came with a raccoon on a leash, Doo! I didn't know that was a raccoon. Talking about, "You don't want it, Black?"

"No, Dad! Why his fingernails like that? That ain't no dog."

racoon

Then he said, "I'm just messing with ya, T. That's a raccoon. We gonna eat him. Do you want some?"

"No, Daddy! I don't want no raccoon." They used to eat all that—raccoon, those rabbits. My daddy used to be taking us on adventures in that St. Bernard Parish, boy.

Pernell: Where did you go?

Tica: Like you had your little snake? My grandma had a real talking parrot. You know how much

money they could have made off the parrot, Doo? My uncles drank liquor, so just imagine the things they had it saying.

Pernell: You'll buy me another snake?

Tica: I don't know. My grandma had 13 children. She used to have her wallet in her bosom and a chain on her refrigerator.

"Grandma, why you got your chain around there?"

"Cause them bitches ain't takin none of my food for them and their wives. They all got jobs. They gonna bring their own meals home. They ain't stealin none of my meat."

grandmother

My mama's mama was cool, too. She sat in Jumonville and smoked white boys [*joints*] cause she had brain surgery. It used to be tripping me out. A lot of older people stayed in her court who grew up together and they still stuck together. When people had dreams, they'd come to her. She told them what they meant. She was right, too.

She had an account at the drug store and when women got abused by their old man or they didn't do for the baby, she sent me to get a pack of Pampers. She used to be fighting the men when they'd come around to explain their case. Soon as they'd go to talking, she'd punch them dead in the mouth—bust their lip: "That's for beating up the girl outside in front of all them fuckin people."

Pernell: For real. What was it like growing up with eight brothers and sisters?

Tica: It just was me for like 12 and a half years. Everything was always serious in the house cause

I was the only child. It was lonely, you know. I had my imaginary friends. [*Laughter*] For real!

When my mama started having the children, I was happy cause I knew I would have somebody to play with, somebody to dress up like a baby doll.

Pernell: Tell me the worst thing you ever saw.

Tica: When I was a teenager, I found my baby brother dead. He was two and a half months going on three. He died from crib death. That's when a baby die in his sleep, when they forget to breathe. And my mom didn't know CPR. She blew in his mouth, gave him to me, and ran across to our neighbor Yolanda who was a nurse. Well, I'm still holding the baby. By then, I'm hearing him catch his last breath—all these sounds you wouldn't expect nobody ain't breathing to make. It gave me a hole in my heart when I was 14.

Pernell: How did you meet my dad?

Tica: Every summer, my mama let me go down to Desire to get away from just helping her with the children every day.

Your daddy was older than me, but he didn't know that cause I was mature—my mama had schooled me from young. She told me what was happening in the streets. I'm glad she did, too—it made me stronger for the world today.

Pernell: What was it like hanging out with someone from the Desire?

Tica: My grandma brought me a .22 to take on the bus when I went down there, but I never had to use it cause I wasn't that type of person to go look for trouble. If somebody tried to say something to front, I'd put them in their place with my mouth.

Pernell: How would you describe the boys in the St. Bernard?

Tica: Some of them are all right. Leaders got their own mind, but some of them are followers, remote control niggas. Press the button and they're on. Some of them are fake, bae.

Pernell: How did you feel when you moved out of your mama's house and got your own apartment in the St. Bernard?

Tica: Relieved, independence. I was on my own. I had my job. We just had you, and your daddy and I had a whole two-bedroom house to ourselves. It was spacious to us.

Tica and Pernell as a baby, courtesy of the Russell family.

Pernell: How old were you when you had me?

Tica: I was 16 when I had you.

Pernell: And how did you feel?

Tica: I don't regret having you, but at the time, I felt like I could have *waited*. I got pregnant right after my brother had done passed while I was still in school. I said, "I don't want to have no babies right now."

Pernell: Did you ever go to jail?

Tica: One night, the police stopped me at the end of the court. I'm 18. They say the police never check women. Yes, they do, cause he checked me four times before he found a matchbox where I put the drugs.

Pernell: What happened when he found the matchbox?

Tica: I went to jail. I didn't say, "It's for him. It's for him," even though it was for your daddy. I acted like it was for me cause it was in my possession. My mom knew this man who worked at rehab, and you had to have some type of drugs in your system to get in. By me smoking weed, I was able to go in there for 30 days. I had to complete the program or my bond was gonna be 100,000 dollars.

Pernell: How did you meet Shank's dad?

Tica: When your daddy went to jail, that's how I met Boo. I was working at McDonald's. Boo was working for City Parkway. And me and Boo just chilled til your daddy came home from jail. That was my one friend. You had told your daddy on the phone that I had a friend named Boo and he cut your hair. You ratted on me.

Tica and Darrell, courtesy of the Russell family.

Pernell: I didn't rat.

Tica: When your daddy came back, I went back and forth but then just chose to go back with your daddy. I felt that was the family thing to do. I remember one time I was getting you ready for the nursery at New Day—you were four. My cousin Darrell was sleeping in your bed, and he jumped up out of sleep cause Boo woke him up trying to get in the house through the window. Darrell putting his feet all over him, "Tica!! You better come get this boy!! I coulda shot him! He gettin in the window!"

See, with Boo I learned it's not always gonna end in your favor, even though you're playing the game. That's why I will only mess with somebody else when I know I'm fully out of a relationship. I'll sit back and settle the pain, the memories—let all that die down—then get me a friend.

A couple of months after I left Boo alone. I found out I was pregnant. I didn't know that the baby was for Boo. I was thinking the baby was for Pernell. [Dad's] When Shank got to be about nine months we found out the truth. It took Pernell a little time to accept it. That really hurt him, but I was hurt, too, for what he done before that. But we were still together. He was working; I was working. When he would buy you something, he would buy Shank something, too. It didn't take the man out of him. We stayed together and a few years later, I was pregnant with Rasheed.

That's when the drugs just came in. He always was a man to work, but the drugs were messing up our relationship. I could see the money difference where his habit was getting stronger. Yeah, he didn't want to let me see the check stub any more.

Our hood always had these drug dealers, but I was never into it until your daddy and me split up. He went to North Carolina for most of my pregnancy with Rasheed, and I started selling drugs, running with the fellas. I took care of y'all like that for six years on my own. Hustling was a whole different world. Nothing's unexpected. You might see users carrying a whole sofa on their back one minute. I'm serious.

It was like I was selling drugs and counseling, because when they came to buy the drugs, they wanted me to listen to their problems. That's why I say, "Everybody's got a story behind em." You never know what turned that person to drugs. It might not be the thrill of drugs. It could be something painful that they're hiding.

Tica's Sons

When I was just a youngun, my brothers and me were known every place we went. At school and in the project, if you knew us, you would say, "Oh, that's Tica's sons right there."

Everywhere we went, we were "fresh." Holidays, all the people would tell me and my brother, "Man, I want those shoes, but my mama ain't had enough," while we had this evil grin on our faces. The whole thing was because my mother sold drugs. She had a job but selling drugs was her main occupation.

When I got to school I would be able to buy anything I wanted—chips, cold drinks. I would pull out my money and stunt. When I made good grades, she would buy me and reward me with shoes, clothes, money, and once, a pocket bike.

She wasn't a big time drug dealer—she just sold every drug you can name, like crack, weed, Xanax, dope, you get the picture. It was fast money but it has consequences behind it. My mama used to have more than 500 dollars in each pocket, but she knew what could happen to her or us if she was to get caught. She complained about the long hours and people trying to steal her customers. But she knew she was nice to them and the male drug dealers used to beat them, so they would always come back to her.

Justin Laird, courtesy of the Russell family.

Justin —one friend

Growing up in the St. Bernard, I had one friend I could tell anything to. His name was Justin Laird. He lived next door to me. My address was 1325 and his was 1327. He was a few years older than me.

We got along really well except for this one time. We were playing cool can and Justin started talking about my grandpa, who had fallen off a third story balcony in the project and died just a few months before. I hit him in the back with a metal bat, and he ran inside and got a knife. We were standing in front of each other and he was crying. His uncle was cool—he knew both of us because he cut hair in the project. He kept telling us to calm down, but his auntie Charo—red with that pretty hair—kept taunting us, "Let em fight! Let em fight!" The next day we were back cool like the other side of the pillow.

A few weeks later, he moved away to Kentucky. We talked on the phone, but not often. When he came back, he was so country. We went to the store and he asked, "Where y'all's pops?" I said, "Cold drinks, Justin, bra!"

He said, "You know what I mean."

One time, after a full day of basketball, we took a shortcut through Lil Phillips Elementary and Justin's brother Byron said, 'Hold on, I'm about to get something."

I said, "What?"

He said, "Just wait for me." I turned around and he picked up the garbage can and broke the window. I said, "Come on, man!" He started ripping up everybody LEAP scores. I look back and before you know it I had a .357 in my face. The police kept saying, 'Get on the ground" so we all laid down. I'm looking at Justin. He's crying and telling Byron, "I'm not following you no more!"

I said to myself, "You dumb for following your lil brother anyway." You know how you put your face to the side when you're on the ground? Byron had his face in the dirt.

Out of the blue, my mother pulled up. Then I saw Justin's mama coming up the street like a Russian bull with a big jailhouse belt. The police told my mama they had to take us to jail. As soon as we got the detention center, it was like the North Pole. They made us take off everything. We walked through the metal detector, they took our belts and shoe strings saying we could strangle someone. As we're going to sleep, I hear Justin and Byron sing 50 Cent's "Many men." We woke up to cold tuna fish and milk.

. We slept there for a few weeks, and I missed my graduation. Then we went to court. My mama had to pay a 140 dollars and their mama had to pay 280. When we got out, Byron said, "That was fun," and his grandma smacked his face off.

When we got back to the St. Bernard, everybody couldn't stop asking us about it. When Eli said, "Let's play football." I was glad for the chance to change the subject. I told them to hold up, I'd go get Justin. As I knocked on the door, I heard this noise. I looked through the window and Byron kept saying over and over, "You ratted on me." Justin said, "You tried to make me take your charge." Byron said, "You're my big brother, you're supposed to." I knocked on the door harder, and Justin came out. We went into the court to choose teams. I told Eli, "I first pick." He said, "I already know, you got Justin."

I went to pick up my trophy for graduation at school. Byron runs up to me and whispers in my ear, "I made everybody in my class pass the LEAP." I couldn't do anything but laugh. We went back to court. I said, "Remember y'all was singing, 'Many Men'?" I should have never said that. He started singing,

Many men wish death upon me
Blood in my eyes, dog, I can't see
I'm trying to be what I'm destined to be
And niggaz trying to take my life away
I put a hole in a nigga for fuckin with me

Over and over.

Trespassing

My daddy moved away to North Carolina and we didn't really talk. I grew up without a father for six months, but it seemed like much longer. I think that's the way I am now is because of all of the break ups between my mother and father. I had to learn everything on my own.

One day I was sitting on my back porch in the project and Justin's mama, Christine, said, "Doo, your daddy is coming up the driveway." I was small, so I stood up on the porch and looked down the driveway. Out of all the people walking, I spotted my daddy. As he got closer and closer, I had butterflies in my stomach and I could not stop myself from smiling. He greeted me with a dap and a hug and said, "I miss you."

Then we walked up the stops and he said, "Where's your mama at?" and I said, "Inside." We got in there and my mama was cooking red beans. He gave her a hug and they started talking. My mama asked him to go to the store.

He said, "Yeah."

He left and didn't come back. I kept thinking I should have walked with him and that maybe he had decided to go home.

He called about a week later and said that the police stopped him by the store and asked him what he was doing back here. He said he was coming to see his son, and he was going to the store for his baby mama. They took him for trespassing.

He moved into some apartments in New Orleans East called Copper Creek and we went over to see him almost every weekend. It was a private apartment complex, so we didn't have to worry about the police.

B.A.C. Maaan

In the St. Bernard, every group of friends had to have a name for themselves. Many were named after Rockafella and Def Jam records—State Property, Dipset, Young Gunz, the Money Tree, and G-Block.

One night, Three and I were running it on the phone and he said, "We need a name for ourselves." We were throwing out options: Paper Chaser, Money Hungry. I called a girl and forgot to click over when I got back on the phone with Three. He proposed another name: "B.A.C." I said, "What that stand for?" He said, "Bad Ass Children." You know we were young, so that sounded cold to us.

The next at day school, the girl's brother came up to me and said, "You like B.A.C., huh, Doo?" And started laughing. I said, "How you know that?" He said, 'Y'all don't know how to work no phone. I heard everything you said last night."

We told the rest of our friends: Tiga, Richard, my uncle, Jamal, and Larry, and we started talking about it in the project and school. A dude named Freddie with State Prop try to battle against me. All I hear I him saying is, "I walked through Foy, I saw them B.A.C. sliding down the pole."

I said the first thing that came to my mind. The whole school never heard me rap—then free styling at that:

State Prop, you gets no props using other people's name.
You could get shot, I'ma let y'all feel the heat.
I'm a drop you like a leaf and
Put you six feet deep.

When there were DJs, The B.A.C. usually got dressed at my house in the Foy court since all of us lived near each other. T-Tiga lived across the court,

Richard and Jamal lived in the next court, and Three, Melvin, Raheem and Roi slept by my house almost every day. We came out fresh: Rocawear jeans, a jersey, a Fitty hat, and the new Jordans—never G-Nikes even though they were the more popular.

When we got to the DJ, the girls were already shaking before the music even started. Since we wanted to be older, we stood by the older guys and danced on girls' booties. Sometimes the girls would dance with us. Sometimes we got slapped.

After an hour, we saw Larry and told him, "Let's go get our motorbikes." He found his friends Gee, Lance, and Terrell, and we got on eight motorbikes, two dirt bikes, and a four wheeler. We passed the DJ as girls were saying, "They need to go ahead! Fuck! People are trying to dance." Even the little children tried to block us by standing on the sidewalks and trying to hit us with sticks.

But we didn't stop: Motorbikes staying on the sidewalk, while the dirt bikes and the four wheeler tore through the court. We rode so fast my eyes teared up.

As soon as the DJ was going good—I mean, people dipping, booty-shaking—someone shot in the air. Everyone scattered screaming and hollering. On our way home, we were laughing and talking about it, making a joke out of everything. "Man, you saw your face? You looked like a sad clown when those bullets started!"

Interview with *Coach* Edward Buckner

Big Ed. When I was young, I would hear all the old dudes come from the park saying, "My coach mean." They had this one dude who would say, "He hit my neck hard with his thumb." I was never the type to play football, but one day I went back there and suited up. And Ed was mean. He yells a lot. I played for a few weeks but one day I woke up and my muscles were so sore from practice that I quit.

But Ed's one of those all around people. He can go anywhere and people know him. During the interview, he talked about how he was homeless. Picture yourself coaching in the day and sleeping in the French Quarter at night. No one ever knew. He also used to have a drug addiction and sold drugs, but he changed his life around and is now the head of the Porch Seventh Ward Cultural Organization.

Edward Buckner outside the Porch Seventh Ward Cultural Organization, by Rachel Breunlin.

Pernell: So where did you grow up?

Ed: I was born and raised, basically, in the St. Bernard Project.

Pernell: How was your childhood there?

Ed: Had a good childhood. I was blessed to have a mother who worked 27 years for the school board. A father who did 21 years in the military, and also worked at City Hall. My parents gave us pretty much everything we wanted. I was a musician and every time I decided to play a new type of percussion instrument, I had a new drum, a new bongo, a new congo. I was trying to even get them to buy me some tympani drums, some big old kettle drums. I finally got them to buy those.

My dad's people come out of Tremé. We was living in the St. Bernard Projects and they would take me up to where they lived to see the second line parades. My uncle, Smokey Johnson, made the tune "It Ain't My Fault"—second line music forever—and my daddy gave me every opportunity to take part. I hardly knew how to dance, but I knew I wanted to be a part of that. My daddy used to call me Soul Brother—his favorite song was "Work, Soul Brother, Work." He was like, "Dance, Soul Brother, dance! Get that, baby. Go ahead on, Soul Brother!" And just had to me all psyched up, second lining and rolling all down the street.

My daddy was in the Dirty Dozen Kazoo Band in the Sixth Ward—he was in the Dirty Dozen *before* they were the Dirty Dozen Brass Band. He was with the

Skulls during Mardi Gras. He would go party and come home at three in the morning having drunk that wine singing Mardi Gras Indian songs, "Ooh nah nay. Ooh nah nay." He was trying to dress me up as an Indian one year, too, and I just cried all day long. Everybody seemed to have scared me to death.

When I got to junior high school age, I went to Bell Junior High School in the Sixth Ward, so I got a chance to meet a whole lot of new people. I ended up finding out later I was family with Lois Andrews and some of those folks. And then going to John McDonogh was another plus because then I knew all the folks from the project *and* from the Sixth Ward. I was a great drum major, but I was just too bad. We had one of the best bands in the whole state in the 70s. But after band practices, I turned back to the Seventh Ward Hard Head thug, running around the school with my Lee jeans hanging down. I thought I could get by being a good drum major, and that didn't work. Folks put me out of they school and I ended up at Carver.

Pernell: Do you think my childhood and yours is different?

Ed: No, cause you come from the same place of origin that I come from. The only thing that's different is that you have more resources now. There's all types of community organizations that can help guide you. Those things weren't as readily available when I was younger. Or, if they were available, it was not a program we were invited to take part in.

The St. Bernard was really a village. People had great understandings of one another. They were great warrior-type, fighting people. They took up social and political measures and would definitely stand up and fight til the end. They lost a lot of battles, but overall the people never lost their pride. The strength of the projects has never been in one individual, but in all of the people.

Pernell: Do you think the St. Bernard is a good place to raise a family?

Ed: Sure. The projects get painted in such a bad picture. When we have a few killers, it tarnished the picture of all the goodness that comes from it, too. The women were the majority in most households, but the coaches at the parks were the daddies. Your grandfather, Melvin Bush, has been a coach for 30 plus years at the playground.

My mishaps in life weren't my parents, they were my choices. I knew that I wasn't supposed to be doing it, but I did them anyway. My parents were about education—about acquiring a better job, being a respectful person in your community. I remember Mr. Omar, the pie man. Every Sunday, Mr. Omar came to our house with a big pie. My daddy just loved patronizing with all of the gentlemen who had little small businesses like that. Every Sunday, he knew that he had some money at our house. And that's one of the reasons why I sell pies now.

Pernell: What day did you move out of the St. Bernard?

Ed: I think I actually never realized I moved. My family moved on Bunker Hill Road in New Orleans East in 1986, but I was there every day because of the coaching. My existence in the St. Bernard Project never came to a proper ending.

Pernell: What was it like coaching football at the St. Bernard?

Ed: Redemption in my life. A return to my community. The wake-up call that I needed to utilize the gift that God has gave me to assemble and organize. Usually when I touch it, it turns to gold. When I was coaching, I became homeless because of the mischievous things that I was doing. Cocaine was hot and all the ladies you wanted were snorting cocaine and drinking. But you're only able to function like that for awhile, because at some point the drug takes prevalence. Instead of going to work, I would use.

And then I stole ten dollars to go get loaded. Nobody ever knew I took the money, but I took it. At that point, I knew I was no good to stay in nobody's house. I had never been a thief, and I found myself looking all around, and wondering who knew I took them the money. I left and went to the street.

I went to the playground to coach and lived on the Riverfront at night. Your grandfather used to give me a ride home every evening. I would tell him I was going to meet my girlfriend at Café du Monde, but I was going to sleep on the Moonwalk steps. The next day, I would wake up and hang out a little bit in the street. And then I'd walk back to the playground to coach football every evening. I had my little bag and everybody thought it was work clothes. I did that for about a year and a half.

Nobody knew I was loaded. I was sweating like a pig and nobody was paying much attention to it. Our team lost every game. We couldn't make a first down. And the next year, I had them same group of boys back, and we got a first down. It was like a miracle. We didn't get a touchdown that year, but when we got a first down, it was like we scored. We partied and talked all night, and then, when I went back to the Moonwalk steps, something hit me: This was not where I wanted to be no more. I needed to be closer to family. I needed to be closer to the team. We were going forward, and I need to be there as a part to go forward.

Pastor Roberts, who is Coach Flea at John McDonogh, was the guy that was the driving force most behind me getting clean off drugs. He gave me the house on N. Villere. But after I got the house, I started smoking and selling again. One night I started thinking, "All that you have to smoke, you about to die. Your life is starting to take a turn for a bad ending." I started walking towards the French Quarter to remind myself of where I used to sleep—where I was headed again if I wasn't careful. And on the steps of a shotgun house on Elysian Fields, I broke down and prayed. I prayed and cried to God to take the crack away from me.

This is like 18 years ago. I never smoked again, but I was still selling, which is just as addictive as smoking because you get to love that money. I sold for about six years before I even got recognized by the police. They raided my house in the Seventh Ward. They kicked in four doors before they got to mine and got me on a witch-hunt. The amount of crack that they caught me selling, it had a ten to 60 year charge on it. You didn't get probation on that charge, it was automatic time.

Of all the people to give me a break, Judge Joe Cannizaro gave me a break. I had coached not just football, but every sport at the playground: football, basketball, baseball, track. You name it, if we had it, I was coaching it. Maybe a year before, it was baseball season and Judge Joe Cannizzaro's son played shortstop. I didn't know he was a judge, I was just talking to him as a parent.

When I went to his court, he recognized me. He said, "Coach, I know you. You're a better man than this." He say, "I'm going to give you an opportunity to set yourself straight. If you don't do drugs or be involved with drugs, I'll give you five years probation. I'm going to test you every week." I didn't have any involvement with selling. A year later, he tested me, brought me in court, and threw out the remaining four years I had on probation. He said that day, "Coach, you're ready."

Pernell: What kind of coach were you?

Ed: I think I was a disciplinarian type coach, which was how I was taught when I was in the band as a drum major. In Mr. Richardson's band at Bell, it was discipline first—then you had the guys listen to you and pay attention. Coaching is a great lesson. Not just for children, it's for adult men, too. Because as much as you are building character with kids, you're actually building a mind set and a lifestyle for yourself. You think you're just having fun, and then all of a sudden you start to realize that you're there for a bigger purpose and that's to train young men to be grown men. Young men to be good daddies. Young men to have respect for one another no matter what they do—throwing trash or being president of the United States.

And, of course, you know I won a lot of championships in football and basketball—citywide championships. And I always told everybody, "I win as a coach, but the community wins as a whole." You're building a winning a concept. My kids were underprivileged kids, so in order to be a good coach, I had to teach my kids that the norm could be winning. And they could have winning in a humble way. When we won, we didn't spite nobody and talk about them. We walked across the field, shook their hand, told them good game. It starts to change the way young men think. That's why I be on you about what you do because I want you to have that same attitude.

Brandon

When my parents stopped talking to each other for good, my mama was single for a long time. My cousin Troy's daddy came by our house with this man with long hair and a baseball cap on. When they were leaving, I overheard my mama telling Troy, "I like him."

A few days later, Troy and the same man came in a car and my mama was talking to the man. She went inside for something and me and my nosey brother ran up to the car. The man asked my cousin, "Those her sons?" He said, "Yeah." He dapped our hands and said, "My name's Bee." I told him my name was Doo. He said, "Iight, man." I was about ten years old when that happened. Later I found out he was Coach Ed's son.

I remember Brandon came around so much that he moved in after about a year. We made this bond between us that nobody could break. One day in the seventh grade I was doing homework, and Bee came and sat on the bed next to me and said, "You think you're going to college?" I said, "No, I want to take up a trade." Then I saw this look on his face like, "Boy, you're crazy." He showed me one of his college tests and was like, "If I could do it, you could do it."

Brandon Dugars in the St. Bernard, courtesy of the Russell family.

Brandon + tica

Interview with My Mom, Part II

I had my own perspective on how Brandon and my mama got together, but I knew there was probably more to the story because our families had known each other for a long time. In the St. Bernard, people are close in ways you might not expect. I laughed at the whole thing. It was pretty funny to hear her side.

Pernell: Tell the story of how you met Brandon, where and when.

Tica: I've been knowing Brandon because I've always known his daddy, Ed Buckner, and his grandma and them. They stayed across the driveway from my grandma. His grandma and my grandma were good friends, but I was older than Brandon. I had you when I was 16, and he was about ten then.

I used to play cards with his auntie and them so I'd see him. He was always a handsome boy with long eyelashes—that curly hair and that crooked leg. He had one bowleg. That was what made me just like him, and I always used to inquire about him, and watched him as he grew up. Once, I had rubbed his leg and told him, "Ooo, I could look for you when you get older." He always remembered that.

But as he got older, his family was moving around and I lost contact with him. Their grandma had passed, and Ed moved out of the projects. I didn't him until he was like 21 and I was 27. He was out of school and in college then.

Brandon, courtesy of the Buckner family.

He was hanging out with my cousin—my cousin and his cousin are cousins—around the house in the hood, but I didn't know that was the same guy from back then.

He gave me his phone number, but I was like, "I don't like him cause he younger." I used to see him around, but I would never call him. He used to always tell my sister Ne Ne, "Tell her to holla." One time I just called him and we were conversating on the phone for a couple of minutes. He came in the projects and we smoked a blunt.

We started talking, and getting closer, and we just started kicking it. He became my honey.

Ne Ne- pernell's
Aunt

59

I'm About to Leave Out of Here

For some reason Justin and I stopped being friends. We would see each other at school and boot up. One day in middle school, I was walking home from detention and something told me to go the long way. I was walking up Senate and saw Justin getting jumped by some dudes out at Parkchester. I jumped in and we got jumped together.

On the way home, we laughed. He told me, "Your eye big." I said, "Dog, your nose busted. Justin, they was kicking the shit out of you!"

He said, "I was happy you came."

"You saw how I snuck that dude with dreads when I got up? What if I would never have came?"

"I would have been looking like Martin."

Later on that day, the kids off my side of the whole Foy and Duplessis courts got some water balloons and went on the other side of the project and found Douglas, Dula, and them. We pitched the balloons at them because we knew they were the only ones who would try to get us back.

Later on, all of us were sitting in the court. Jamal said, "That look like Dula and em." Henry said, "Stop spookin." As they got closer, I ran through the cut to see. It *was* them all right and they didn't have water

balloons. They had rocks. Big rocks. As I ran back, I tapped Justin on the leg and he started running behind me. All I could hear were rocks hitting the wall. I stopped and looked back. Chopec had fallen and Nardo hit him in the back with a bike tire. Then a rock hit me in the chest. Justin pulled my shirt and said, "Come on, man."

I saw Dula at school the next day. He told me, "I'm gonna get you." I said, "Iight." After school, Justin and I were walking when Dula threw some muddy water on us. He was Forrest Gump that day—we ran him all the way to the other side of the project, but I couldn't catch him. As we were walking home, everyone was saying, "Y'all stink."

When I got home, I got a whipping. In the tub, I was saying to myself, "I'm gonna get Dula tomorrow." But when I got there, the principal and the whole school was by the front gate. He said, "No school. Hurricane watch." Everybody ran to the project—like 200 people. I did not even care about getting Dula back.

The next day, it was raining on and off. All the corner stores were crowded and some you couldn't even get in. Riot people were going crazy. I mean,

whole family

when we got in the stores everything was gone. We had to drive far away to get food and supplies to wait it out. Bee and I stayed up watching the news in the wee wee hours of the night. In the morning, the storm touched down. Ten minutes later, the power went out. I looked out the window across the driveway to my friend Richard's apartment. I clicked the flashlight once and he clicked it back.

It rained for a long, long time. After the rain, everyone started coming out. I sat on the porch with all my friends talking about, "When y'all think the lights gonna come back on?" My mama called me and told me they just broke into King's. My friends and I flew around there. As we ran, I was looking at the fallen power lines, window panes gone. We got to the store and you couldn't see anything out in the darkness. I heard Justin say, "Say Doo, where you at?" I said, "I'm about to leave out of here." He said, "Come on."

The only thing we got was a box of candles. The water was getting higher and higher and the sun was starting to go down.

The next morning the water was only a few feet away from our second floor. My mama and Bee decided we needed to go. Shank, Melvin, and I swam. Bee had Rasheed on his neck. Bee was holding my mama's hand and she was holding onto to her sisters'. We slept in an abandoned apartment that was much higher than ours. The next day, we saw our cousin Kelly paddling on an air mattress. He took Shank, my grandma, and her son Kelvin to the interstate. They met some white men with boats who came back to get us.

SAVE
PUBLIC HOUSING
NO DEMOLITION

The St. Bernard Public Housing Development, Post Katrina, by Pernell Russell.

PART II: EXILE & RETURN

Pernell: Even after the St. Bernard flooded, I thought I was coming right back home.

Daron: I cleaned up my room. I said, "When I come back, I don't want to have none of this to do!"

Pernell: After we evacuated and were on the bus, I fell asleep. When I woke up, I'm rubbing my eyes and I see a sign for Houston. I said, "Ma, where we at?" "Houston." "Bee?" "Yeah, we're in Houston, dawg." "What?!" We get to the Astrodome, man—

Daron: We drove around there to find my Auntie Tasha and them, but they weren't there. My mama took some other people back to our hotel.

Pernell: Son, we looked around, saw all the cots and people. Brandon said, "I can't sleep in here." I said, "Me neither." We walked around until we found a hotel. When we first moved in, cars were stopping giving us money. One lady was crying. That's how we got sponsored by Ms. E. She started bringing us different places, showing where things are.

Daron: A lady came to our hotel where there were New Orleans people staying. She gave my mom 200 dollars and asked what else she needed. My mama was like, "A microwave," so she went to Walmart and bought her one and came back. She was in the hallway in the hotel talking, and my mama was crying. That's when it hit me. I started seeing the water and people on the buildings. "Man, my city gone!"

Pernell: I was mad!

Daron: The manager at the hotel offered for us to stay at her house, but my mama found an apartment.

Pernell: We stayed off of South Port Oaks.

Daron: Everybody from New Orleans was moving in there, and everyone from Houston was moving out.

Pernell: Where I stayed, we were townhouses. All the New Orleans people stayed way in the back and all the Houston people stayed in the front. It was like a little project.

Daron: They called us refugees.

Pernell: They acted like we came from another country. That made Al Sharpton mad: "Stop calling them refugees! They are still American citizens!"

Daron: The younger people were into all that Blood and Crips.

Pernell: Yeah, man, get away from me with all that!

Daron: I thought that was in California. I saw one guy and I was like, "Man, you must really like red," and he's like, "I've got to wear it." And if a Blood wears blue, they've got to wear a—

Pernell: Band-aid on it.

Daron: It's not that different than New Orleans.

Pernell: Yes, it is!

Daron: Well, we've got cliques in New Orleans that are like gangs!

Pernell: No they're not, son. In Houston, you got to get jumped in to get into their clique. We don't have to do all that. That's stupid. Why would I beat up my lil partners to be in a clique? I went to this school called Jones. When we get to school—it's like three bus loads of New Orleans people—all we see is them putting their hands up, making the H. We're like, "What they doing that for?" That stands for Houston.

Daron: In the morning time, New Orleans used to be so deep. We sat on the floor in the hallway. There were so many of us, people had to walk over us.

MOVING BACK

Pernell: I was gone my whole eighth grade year and I started ninth grade and then came down here. All my aunties and my grandma were down here. My aunties were telling me, "We go to John Mac." I said, "Oh, I got to get to the Mac!"

Daron: When we were first back, we were living with my cousin across the river. It was two bedrooms.

Pernell: I used to hate that, son—living with people. The first house we found, we snatched it.

Daron: I missed the projects, but—

Pernell: At that time, we were thinking they were going to open the projects back up. At first they didn't have any gates around the buildings, so we still used to be in there. And then when they put up the chain link fences, that still didn't stop us because everybody went to Willie Hall Park nearby.

Daron: When we drove around there, all the gates were up. I stood on the gate and looked at my courtway.

Pernell: You were having flashbacks?

Daron: I was having visions of everything that used to happen back there. Like I was watching myself playing in the court.

Pernell: I was having beaucoup flashbacks. But now I like that peace and quiet around my house. I like that. That's why my daddy moved to the suburbs way back in Terrytown!

Photograph of Daron at his house in the East, by Pernell Russell.

Daron

New Part of the Family

Aunt Tasha

We were in Houston and my mama was worried about her baby sister, my auntie Tasha. My mama knew she had stayed with her boyfriend Travis and her son, Greg, but we hadn't heard from them. She was in the hotel room watching the news, and she was trying to call anyone she knew who might have known where they were. She couldn't get through and was crying and worried.

Finally we got a phone call. They were in Austin. They had to leave the flooded Calliope and swim to the Superdome. Travis started to worry about his mom, and swam back by Xavier University to make sure she was okay. She had already left so he swam back to the Superdome to wait on the buses.

We drove to pick them up. They looked very tired and worn out, so we turned around immediately and drove back to the hotel that we were at in Houston. The next morning my parents took them to the Astrodome to get their tetanus shots. We heard that they were giving out housing vouchers, so my mom and aunt went to pick them up. We moved into an apartment complex not too far from my school. We lived directly in the middle and Travis and Tasha lived closer to the front.

Tasha had been with Travis for about a year. We knew him a little bit, but living together in Houston he became more like family. Travis is a very cool person. He's funny, smart, and is all about the dollar, but has a big heart

Text messages went around to everybody's phones saying that FEMA (Federal Emergency Management Agency) was giving families 10,000 dollars each. My mom and my aunt woke up bright and early the next morning to stand in the line to fill out for the emergency money. There is no word to describe how long the lines were. They told them the check would be mailed.

We had a family meeting in the living room—my mom, my dad, my brother, my sister, and me. My mom and dad told us to write down everything we needed like underclothes, shoes, and uniforms. Then we started talking about what else we could do with the money. My dad said, "We are going to buy the t-shirt machine so we can start selling New Orleans style t-shirts for parties. Plus we need the paper and t-shirts to go with the machine."

We decided to use the rest of the money on equipment for a home studio. Every day that the mailman passed, I would run to the mailbox like a bunch of kids running after an ice cream truck.

A couple of days after getting our FEMA check, my mom and dad walked through the door with a couple of large boxes. We all rushed to the living room and attempted to open them until my dad said, "Is y'all crazy? Get your hands off my stuff." When he opened the boxes, I was so excited—it was a brand new keyboard, mic, speakers, and laptop.

One day we went by Tasha's apartment and saw the same kind of equipment. We asked, "Who that's for?" Travis said, "That's for me." My dad said, "I didn't know you was into music."

Travis, "Yeah, man, I been doing this."

Travis, aka T-Sibley, was the man behind the best beats we would ever hear.

The T-Shirt Machine

The first few t-shirts we did for free. We made them for three people in our apartment complex who were going to a birthday party. They asked us to put their picture next to the person's whose birthday is was. After people saw our graphics, more and more people started asking how much we were selling them for. Depending what they wanted on the shirt, and what size shirt, we began to figure out prices.

At first, my mom was buying the t-shirts out of the store. Then she went to get her wholesale license and was getting big boxes of t-shirts for little or nothing and we started seeing more profits. We were making more than just RIP and Happy Birthday shirts. My mama and I came up with different designs. One had a cereal bowl with weed in it and it said, "Weed Loops." Another had the Pillsbury Dough Boy with beaucoup money in his hand, and it said, "Dough Boy." I used to take them to the car wash right across the street from where we were living. In no time, I would sell them all.

Home Studio

Our t-shirt machine was set up in the dining room of our apartment. The living room was our home studio. We had the laptop on a side table near a big window with one speaker on each side. The wires ran from the living room to the closet, which was the booth. Inside the closet, we put sound proof foam around the walls and everybody who ever rapped in the booth signed their name on the door when they finished recording their song.

It felt so good keeping money in our pocket instead of having to pay 50 dollars an hour in someone else's studio. T-Sibley and my dad, Chevy Earnhard, started collaborating. Travis would make a beat, and if my daddy heard that he needed another sound, he'd add on to it.

I had just started rapping and wasn't used to staying up all night, so I would sit on the sofa and fall asleep in the middle of every studio session. But after awhile, I started realizing that T-Sibley is a master mind. The way that he combines the instruments together, it's like he's a musical genius. I am very glad to have somebody like him on my team. If I was trying to buy a beat like Sibley makes from somebody else, the price would be at least 300 dollars. How does he do it? I wouldn't be able to tell you because I don't know myself. He lets his hands do the talking for him.

Show in New Orleans

One day when we were in the studio mixing down our Street Money mixtape, we got a phone call from my uncle Zack saying that he was having a party at the bar in New Orleans—uptown on Liberty Street—and wanted my dad and cousin to perform. I was so excited about it and they were hyped. My dad got off of the phone and said:

Dad: Man, it's on and popping. I want to go all out for this.
Cousin: What do you mean go all out?
Dad: I'm saying I want our mixtapes printed, I want our label t-shirts made, and I want to give them a show like they've never seen before.
Cousin: That's what's up. I want to be fresh.
Dad: Real!
Me: Man, I'm gonna show y'all how the big dogs get down on stage.
Dad: Too bad you're too young. Ha ha.
Me: Are you serious? Man, my name's Money. I know they're going to let me in.
Dad: Ha ha ha! That shit don't work everywhere, but I'm going call Zack and see what's up.
Me: Man, they would want to let me in there. I'm too cold to be left out.
Cousin: What is your fat ass trying to say about us?
Me: Man, I ain't saying y'all ain't cold, but I'm a dog.
Dad: You're really funny, you know that?

Me: What do you mean, "I'm funny"?
Dad: First of all, get your age up, then start comparing yourself to us.
Cousin: Ha ha ha ha.
Me: What are you laughing at?
Cousin: Your young ass. Ha ha.
Me: I can't wait until I turn 18–I'm gonna rock every show at every club like a big dog's supposed to.
Dad: If you say so.

The mixtapes were printed, the t-shirts were printed, now all they had to do was go to N.O. and give a good show. I sat up all night watching T.V. and kept calling my mama asking how it was going. She said, "It's going good. Stop aggravating me and let me enjoy it."

My dad and David, *→ mother's cousin* my mama's cousin, performed a song called "Street Money." By the end of the show everybody was screaming, "It's Street Money nigga!" Everybody had on the Street Money shirts we made and were asking for them to do shows at their parties.

When my dad came home, he was so excited he started to work on copyrighting our label and our names. When we found out that Street Money was already taken, it took us awhile to come up with a new name.

71

Under Control

My mom and dad called me into their room. They said they had a question to ask me.

Dad: Say, bra, real shit—if we were to leave y'all out here during the week while we go work back home, do you think you gonna be able to handle it?

Me: Ummmm, I guess. Why y'all going to work out there?

Mom: You guess? You're 16 years old. You're supposed to know.

Me: Yeah, I could handle it.

Dad: We really need you to be very responsible and be a big brother.

Mom: Serious shit, because I don't need to be all the way in New Orleans worrying about if y'all at school or if y'all fighting and the police come get y'all because y'all home alone.

Me: Ok, I got y'all. I promise.

Even though I was telling my mom and dad that I had everything under control, and that I was going to handle it, inside I was a little worried. Worried about how my brother and sister were going to act towards me once my mom and dad were gone. I didn't want my mama to know that I was worried because that was going to make her worried, so I didn't say anything.

They found jobs in a part of Jefferson Parish called Shrewsbury. I had no idea where that was. My daddy was working at a rug cleaning company and my mama was working at McDonald's. They told me they'd stay with relatives.

Once my mom and dad were getting ready to leave, I could see it in my brother's and sister's eyes that they were going to act a fool the moment our parents walked out the door. I went in my mom's room to ask her to talk to my brother and sister to let them know that I was in charge while they were gone. I was hoping that the talk was going to work, but an hour after mom and dad left, my brother and sister went to fighting over a chair.

I grabbed my brother and told him, "Just give her the chair, she's a girl."

He told me, "You can't tell me what to do. You ain't my daddy!" At that point in time, I wished I was his daddy so I could whip his ass. I figured that it was going to take them a minute to get used to me being in charge.

Every morning, I set my alarm for 6:00 a.m.. My brother's bus passed at 7:02 a.m.. I had to get him up, help him get dressed, and make sure that he made it to the bus stop every morning, then had to rush back home to hop in the shower to be at school by 8:00 a.m..

At first it was hard, but as days went by, it got easy. I had to come help my brother with his homework, make sure he took a bath, and then get my homework done. Mom had cooked for the week, so all I had to do was warm the food. I did this for a month strong.

The Calliope fenced off, by Daron Crawford.

Moving Back

I didn't think that my mom was going to ever want to move back home. I could tell that my mom and dad were starting to get tired from driving back and forth from N.O. to Houston...and from Houston to N.O. One weekend she came home and told us to pack our clothes—that we were moving back home. I had gotten so used to living in Houston that I wasn't too excited about moving back.

When it came about that we were going to move, we were low on funds and nobody had a job so we pawned all of the equipment so that we could get back home. Travis kept a few pieces of his equipment. We packed up as much as we could and had plans to make a second trip for everything else, which never happened. We left a big screen television, our bed frames, the microphone, and my XBox.

The whole ride back home I couldn't say anything because I was thinking about what I was going to see. This was the first time I had ever returned. When we made it in the city, everything looked so old and broken down. The streets looked dead and there were watermarks on every building and house. Stores were locked up and a lot of houses were torn down.

It didn't really hit me until we took a ride through the Calliope Projects. Riding past my old neighborhood, everything was gated up. I tried to envision all of the people that used to be outside in the courtway, under the tree, and on the porch.

I stood at the gate that surrounded my court, watching myself play football with Darnell and the rest of the project, when my mom told me it was time to go. Darnell and his family had decided to stay for the hurricane and I haven't heard from him since. I wish there was a way to get in touch it him. I tried searching MySpace but had no luck.

I remembered the days when I could just stand in the middle of the court and scream his name and he would come running from around the building like a wild horse. Now if I go stand in the court, all around me there's just pieces of bricks and the call of his name just echoes.

73

The East

My parents found a house in New Orleans East in the newspaper soon after we came back. It was something new to me because I had never been in that part of the city before. I never had been around people from the East, and thought it was some kind of rich neighborhood. It had taken in a lot of water during Katrina. When we moved back there, it was very quiet and dark. The block that I moved onto, Lynhuber Drive, didn't have anyone but us living on it when we first moved in. Our landlord, an old drunk man, had fixed up his own house around the corner.

It was just our two houses for awhile. It stayed isolated for three months before we finally got next-door neighbors, David and his grandmother. They had lived in the Ninth Ward before the storm and their house had flooded, too. David was my age, a cool dude, but he was a fighter. Neither one of us knew a lot about the East, but as time went on, the block started to fill up. It seemed like every day we

were driving home, a new family had moved onto the block.

People were moving back to New Orleans from Houston, Atlanta, and Dallas. Many returned home with not much at all, and others returned with the furniture received from FEMA. Most of the older people who moved onto our block returned to homes they owned and had rebuilt. There were a few trailers on the block as people were living in them to rebuild.

The other people who were coming back were people who had lived in the projects, and now were renting homes—you could tell who had lived in the project by the way they dressed and talked: sagging pants and hood slang like, "What's good" and "Say, son."

I had gotten used to not hearing gunshots, but then one night on the block behind my house 20 shots rang out.

My mom didn't have much to say, but, "Oh! It's time to get from around here."

Interview with My Mom, Part II

When we came back from Houston, my ma felt like it was a step forward not being in the project anymore. When we found out that most of the Calliope wasn't going to reopen, she said, "It really doesn't make a difference because we're not moving back in there anyway." At first, I really wanted to go back because I couldn't see myself living anywhere else. The East felt like the desert, it was real dead. My ma said, "It's better than them damn projects."

I did this interview with my mama to see how she really felt on the inside about moving back home. When I told her I needed to interview her she seemed very nervous. She asked me all types of questions about what I was going to ask her and what it was for, but once I started interviewing she calmed down and seemed very open.

Daron: How did Katrina affect you?

Melvina: I would say Katrina was a blessing. I mean, not to all people and I feel sorry for the people who lost their lives and all. But for me, coming from the Calliope and being able to be somewhere else and look back on the way we were living. Being on the inside, I don't think I would ever notice, but being on the outside I could see pretty much what it is—drugs, violence, all in this little square. No one wanted to go anywhere because they're scared of the light bill, water bill. They didn't want to get a job because they didn't want the rent to go up, you know. Our kids didn't deserve that.

It's made me stronger because there we were paying 50 to a 100 dollars in rent. Sucking up mildew, not having too much privacy. Now we're in some-body else's home, but it's a step up from the projects because we are actually getting out there working hard for what we want. We pay 1,000 dollars rent to somebody to live in their home, and it's making us say, "Well, what we're paying, this is a house note and some." It hurts sometimes that we can't give y'all the things that you really do deserve and need, but I really think y'all appreciate us as parents that we are today.

Daron: What made you move back to the city after Katrina?

Melvina: Needing a job. Needing to be able to take care of y'all. I mean, we were getting unemployment, we got a lump sum from FEMA, but we had to catch up on the insurance, and travel back and forward trying to get a job and find somewhere to stay. That took a lot so we were back to zero.

Daron: Do you regret moving back to the city?

Melvina: Not this time.

Daron: What do you do for a living now?

Melvina: I drive a school bus. I love my job. I have some bad ass kids, but they're wonderful.

Daron: Can you describe a afternoon being on the bus with kids going home from school?

Melvina: It's not so hard. Once you park the bus, you take this deep breath in, and you feel good because you've had all these kids' lives in your hands. You got them all to their destination safe without any incidents, so it makes you feel good and look forward to the next day.

Daron: Can you give us a story about one day on the bus? [*Laughter*]

Melvina: Yeah. We have three brothers from Basin and Bienville in the Iberville Housing Development, and all they talk about is gangsta this and rapping that, and they want to have their pants sagging. They're little kids. I have to tell them, "If you're gonna ride the bus, you need to fix your clothes, say good morning, say good evening." I ask them how their day is going. But the oldest out the three is about 12 and he's just so mannish. When you look at him, it's like you're looking at a short grown person.

This particular morning, I passed and they weren't at the stop, so I waited. I've been making that stop at 7:00 a.m. for two months. I wait five minutes to see if they're gonna come out their door. They didn't come and I called in to base and let them know. Twenty minutes later base calls me, "Driver, you need to go back." By now, I'm way in Carrollton picking up another kid.

At 7:30, I'm back and the 12 year old comes onto the bus. I overheard him tell one of the other little students how he was watching the cartoons, how the bus is gonna wait on him. I said, "Well, what were you doing that you couldn't make it to the stop?" And he said, "I was just chillin, Ms. Mel, you know how it be." I'm like, "Explain chillin to me. Were you chillin waiting on your brothers to get ready?" He's like, "No, you know how it be, it's still dark out in the morning and I can't be coming out here."

I said, "Well, where is the thug in you now? You scared of the dark?" [*Laughter*]

All the kids on the bus were laughing and he felt played. He went and told his mom, and his mom and I had to go into the office. All of them don't have good understanding moms. Some can be pretty hard to deal with.

Daron: What do you like to do for fun?

Melvina: I love to take pictures of my kids. I love to catch y'all smiling at your happiest because I want y'all to have that as you get older to show your kids. We didn't have all of that. I was the only girl who played football for McDonogh 28. They suited me up and everything. I actually played with the boys, and I have no pictures. I had a most valuable player trophy, and my little brother broke it. I went to the school to try to get pictures, and they had none. I said I wanted to keep these pictures of y'all at your best.

Daron: Thanks, Mom.

Melvina: Thank you. It was emotional. And then you wouldn't tell me nothing of what you were gonna ask.

Daron: I wanted it to be a surprise

Melvina: This was very uplifting, though, I liked this.

Life Music

Once we were all back into New Orleans, Aunt Tasha got an apartment in Uptown on Jackson and Travis got an apartment in Metarie for the studio. It was a nice apartment past Elmwood Mall.

After school and on the weekends, my dad and I would go over to work on music. Being in the studio felt like Houston—it was the same kind of apartment complex that we all stayed in, but quieter. His computer was on a stand with the beat machine right to the side. The booth was still a closet.

Chevy Earnhard and T-Sibley were like the old Jay-Z and Dame—Dash. They became a power team with my dad rapping about his past and what he about now and T-Sibley's beats a mix of Southern and West Coast rhythm: a hard hitting, slow-riding beat.

We spent so much time together my dad and Travis decided to start their own record label, "Beat Box Music Group." My dad went up to Tipitina's, where they had a resource center for musicians after Katrina, and met a lawyer who helped them set up the business. He told me I would be the first artist signed.

I didn't waste any time signing on all the Xs. My dad told me, "I know that it might not ever happen, but, if you ever want to leave the company, I'll sign off on it." I felt like he respected me as an artist and not just his son. Like usual, he was supportive, but not pushy.

Travis got tired of living in an apartment and moved into a house in Shrewsbury. His house was much bigger and the studio looked ten times better.

We now have three monitors, a keyboard, a mixing board, a beat machine, and a much bigger booth. The studio that we have now brings better music out of us because it is so much more comfortable.

Besides us, some of Chevy Earnhard's and Travis's friends they grew up with come by to rap: Boo, Greatness, Profit, St. Louis. From hanging out with them, I've learned how to expand what I'm rapping about. They're storytellers. When they're rapping, the sound comes through the computer. Tales of life's downfalls fill the room: Profit's stories of a girl who had to sell her body to eat every day or a boy who lost his daddy so he started selling drugs and got killed. One of my favorite comes from my dad with a kicky ending: A man gambling at the casino is winning big while somebody's watching him. They send someone to kidnap his son and mail a ransom letter to the mama. The song ends with my daddy saying, "The ultimate death was the cost/kidnapper got a call that the dad just lost."

Interview with
My Dad, Part II

It's like this man invented money. If he didn't have anything else to live for, he'd die trying to get money. When it comes to money, that man is the ultimate hustler. He can buy something from you and sell it back to you for double the price and I bet you would buy it. He's like a human calculator. If we are about to order food, by the time we get to the register, he already knows our total, including the tax.

My dad does everything to get money. He works as a manager at a restaurant. He buys stock, he's a real estate agent, and he runs Beat Box. We've made a mix tape called "Chevy Boyz" that features my dad and me (aka Chevy Earnhard and Money) and special guests Profit, Boo, and Greatness. My dad and T-Sibley printed a thousand CDs. On the cover is two Chevys facing each other. We sell them on the street—at gas stations, at school, and work.

If there's anything you need to know about the business side of rap, just ask him and I guarantee that he is right 99.9% of the time. He feels that his family deserves the finer things in life, and I'm not talking about video games and nice tennis shoes. I'm talking about a nice home and being able to afford to send all three of his kids to go to college. I interviewed my dad to find out how it feels to make legal money, what his motivations are, and why he has so many different jobs.

nickname

Roderick Gordon, aka Chevy Earnhard, by Lindsey Darnell.

78

Daron: What do you do for a living? *brother in law*

Roderick Right now I'm a manager of a restaurant. ✻ *brother in law* Also, my brother-in-law, Travis (aka T-Sibley), and I have an entertainment company called Beat Box Music Group. It's been in the works for a while, but it took awhile to do all the paper work. My wife and I also have a mobile detailing service, and I also hold a real estate license with which I practice real estate from time to time.

I'm chasing money in the positive manner. It's just like being in the hood, you've got to explore all options. You can never get all your revenue from one source.

Daron:: Do you enjoy what you do?

Roderick Yeah, of course I enjoy what I do. Anything I'm involved with, I got to enjoy what I do cause I want to learn everything about it—the in's, the out's, so I can control my own destiny pretty much. I don't want to be a slave to nobody where my success is limited to what somebody else teaches me or allows me to do.

Daron:: What do you do in your spare time?

Roderick: In my spare time I try and make tracks—sit around and free style, and play with my kids.

Daron: Where do you see yourself in ten years?

Roderick: Oh man, in ten years I see myself as a music mogul, multi-million dollar man. Having an empire: real estate, successful music company, being a successful artist with a roster of other successful artists. I have a plan, in five years, to have a million dollars. In ten years, hopefully, I'll have ten million.

Daron: If there was one thing in your life that you could change, what would that be?

Roderick: I wouldn't change anything in my life. Everything that happened to me made me who I am. If half of the things wouldn't have happened, I wouldn't have nothing to rap about. I wouldn't have business experience that I have. I would just have been somebody who walked the straight and narrow—went to school, went to college, got a nice little job, but was out of touch with reality. You've got to have a balance between reality and fantasy. I view the "perfect life" as a fantasy. I don't think you can ever have a perfect life. With that being said, I like my life.

Daron at work at Cane's, by Abram Himelstein.

Cane's

On my 16th birthday, May 3, 2007, my dad gave me an application for Raising Cane's as a present and told me I had an interview for four o'clock that day. At first I was like, "Man! Are you serious?"

I was very nervous on my way to the interview after school. I didn't have time to change out of my school uniform. The manager, Dave, was very cool and calmed me down. He asked me two questions: "Is this your first job?" and "Do you want to start working today?" By it being my birthday, I asked him if it was cool for me to start working the following day, and we ended the conversation saying, "See you tomorrow at four o'clock."

The next day I rushed to work right after school. On the bus, the closer we got, the faster my heart started beating. I jumped off the bus on Veteran's Memorial Boulevard, crossing four lanes of traffic, winding my way past the cars, through the parking lot into Cane's 22. Dave introduced me to Gabby, who showed me around. I couldn't help but notice the 250 dollar shoes she had on her feet. I thought everybody wore new shoes to work so I tried it for about two weeks and damaged five pairs of shoes. I started thinking I didn't have that type of money to be spending on shoes to work in, so that "fresh at work" idea ended quick. But Gabby and I became cool. We were both young crew members and by the looks of it, she liked to be fly.

Three months passed and she got promoted to the manager at the Cane's 29 at Lakeside Mall and I moved over there. The restaurant at the mall looked like a car garage, but it was much more fun. Everyday I worked, I saw somebody I knew from school shopping. During the week, I'm worn out, but when payday gets here, just seeing that check makes me full of energy all over again. I used to wonder a lot about how it feels to be grown, and now that I see, being grown it's not all that it seems to be.

When I was a kid, I never knew anything about bills, so I used to ask my parents to buy me this and that. Now that I see my parents struggling to pay some of the bills, I wish that I could give all of the things that I ever begged for back. Bills feel like they just keep coming and coming and we barely have enough to last us until the next paycheck.

It took a little minute, but my family is getting used to not having money to blow, and is realizing that you have to save and invest. I used to spend the money my parents gave me on all of the things that I want. Now that I see money as something that goes really fast, I spend my money on all of the things that I need.

When it's time for bills to be paid, I take care of the water bill and my parents handle the rest. My parents tell and show me how much they appreciate what I am doing. My mother pulls me to the side and tells me, "You're becoming a man," because she knew if she said it around my dad, he would say in a joking manner, "Don't think you're too old to get your ass whipped."

Photograph of Pernell near the St. Bernard, by Abram Himelstein.

Pernell

People may think money is the pursuit of happiness. What's that old saying? More money, more problems. I think people shouldn't chase money because it will run away from you—just like when you chase a girl, she runs. Just like when you snatch water out the river, it runs through your hands.

Tica in Houston, courtesy of the Russell family.

Interview with My Mom, Part II

The storm really made me go crazy. In Houston, nobody could tell me nothing. When we first got our house, we moved into a neighborhood called Clarke Springs. It was furnished down to the detergent and the wig brushes. The next morning, I went outside. It seemed like everybody was from the N.O.

I wanted to go home. I hadn't spent much time out of the city. I went to visit my uncles in Hunts State Penitentiary, I went horse back riding in Mississippi and to Walt Disney World with a summer camp called Excel that was connected to Phillips Junior High. But that was it. In Houston, I didn't

like how everything was so spread out. In New Orleans, you can walk just about everywhere, but there, it's all about the car. We always got lost. My mama was being sponsored by a woman named Ms. E. We used the FEMA money to get a used red Grand Prix. Once we had the car, my mama drove her mom and sisters around to get set up. We made sure we weren't that far away from each other, and we learned our way back and forth.

I interviewed my mama about her perspective after Katrina. I wanted to know how she felt about being responsible for so many of us after the storm.

Tica: After Katrina, I stopped selling drugs. In Houston if you were selling and had children, they would take you to jail, take your children, and put them in the state system, forever. Ms. E, our sponsor, worked in a group home in the state system and I got to see her workplace first hand. I didn't like thinking about my kids in there.

After how we survived Katrina—Bee got the children on his neck, we're holding hands, hopping to the next house cause the water's coming in our own—if something would have happened to one of my children out there, I probably wouldn't be here having this interview because I would have clicked out. My state of mind wasn't together after Katrina.

I was trying to get y'all all your games, get your bikes, four-wheelers, motor bikes, put the sofa in the garage, put another bed in the garage, put the TV in the garage so they could have somewhere to hang out. Let the company come over so they could be where I could watch them. I was doing everything that I could do to keep them out of trouble.

Pernell: Yeah. For real.

Tica: After the FEMA money was gone, we learned about how you got to sacrifice—getting what you need and not what you want. Oh, you didn't like that. You liked the fast money where I'm gonna get everything for the children. Even other people's children—if I got it and I can help them, I'll give it to em. I always felt my conscience from selling drugs.

Franklin Avenue in the Eighth Ward. The Russells' apartment was on the middle left. Photograph by Rachel Breunlin.

Coming Back Home

When I was coming home, I was seeing the same thing over and over: bird, water, bridge, field, field, bird, water, bridge. We were doing almost a hundred on I-10 and the hum of the car made me sleepy. Every time I drifted off, I heard this beeping noise and the car would slow down. It was a scanner telling us when a police was in range.

Finally I saw a sign that said, "New Orleans 54 miles."

I said, "We're almost there. I can't wait until we get in the city." My mama went off on me. "When you get out here you better not change and follow the wrong crowd. If you do, I'ma show you." She already knew what was going on in the city with the murder rate. I looked at her and then reached in the cooler and pulled out a Dr. Pepper. Brandon didn't co-sign. He just kept quiet.

When we got to New Orleans, the first thing I noticed were the X's with numbers on every house. Everything was hard living. With the income tax refund, we got a half a shotgun double on Franklin Avenue. Being on the Ave, I met and saw a lot of people. My mama liked it because it was close to stores. But I had never lived in a house like that before, walking through each room to get to another one, and after a few months I didn't like it—no privacy.

Fence around the St. Bernard Project, by Pernell Russell.

SBM

In June of 2007, I was passing the project, and my mama and I saw people cleaning out their houses. We called all her friends and my friends and told them to come help. My house was on the first floor so it flooded. I was cleaning my room and throwing everything away. I thought about my stash and found my little hole in the wall by my bed. The 20 dollars I hid two years before was still there.

We finished cleaning up and people started barbecuing and playing music. My friends and I started a football game. It was the Old Side versus the New Side. The older men were playing, too. Before you knew it, it was like the whole project was back there.

All of my friends are from different parts of the St. Bernard. My little partner, Jamal, he's out of Jumonville. My uncle Melvin, he's from the other side on Hamburg. My little partner Tee, he's out the green top; and Dee Dee, he's out the baseball court. We decided to make a name for ourselves. Melvin came up with S.B.M. Jamal asked, "What that means?"

Melvin said, "St. Bernard Mob, fool."

& Uncle Melvin

Jamal said, "That's what up. Y'all gonna stay true to it?" Everybody said, "Early!!!!"

Charles, who stayed out of Foy with me, said, "Slug, he not gonna stay true."

Slug said, "Your mama." Everybody laughed.

I was like, "I'm gonna be the president." Melvin said he was going to be the Hitman. Sometimes he doesn't have feelings for nobody.

After the game was over, everybody went their separate ways. My mama asked me when I got home, "You had fun?"

I said, "Yeah, while it lasted."

She said, "You will see them again." I did see my lil homies from time to time, but the S.B.M. broke up because we were scattered. The St. Bernard Projects is still my home.

Pit Bulls

I had a lot of pets over the years: a chow, a ball python, three garden snakes, rabbits, iguanas, guinea pigs, a cat. Some escaped, some we gave away, my mama sold the iguana because she was scared of him, and my dog was hit by a car.

Back in the city, I wanted to get a pit bull, which I believe is the best kind of dog you can have. I like how big their head and muscles can get, and how they will listen to you.

My first dog was 800 dollars. My mama's sister has money because she's always worked. She gave it to me and know she wanted to see the report card. I bought my dog off a man in the Eighth and showed it to my mama. She said, "It gonna get big." I said to myself, "Here she go." She started preaching about, "If you don't take care of him, I'ma put him out."

I run my dog every day. Feed him twice a day, give him a bath every Saturday. Every block I go on from Roman to Spain to Mandeville people will say, "Sell that dog."

Negative people say, "Let's Mike Vick them things!"

I tell them, "I ain't gonna be able to do it."

But when I go to Spain Street? That's my strip. People treat me like a superstar. They ask me what his name is, a million other questions about his bloodline, and how old he is and what his name is.

I tell them, "Akiy."

"Akiy?"

"That's an Indian name."

Pernell and Akiy, by Terrance "T-Tiga" Alford.

My Second Dog

T-Tiga lived just down the street from me. When we wandered around the Eighth Ward, we saw this man walking a grey pit bull around. I heard Tiga say, "That's a blue pit."

I said, "A blue pit?"

And the man said, "Yeah, a blue pit. Their eyes and their nose be blue."

I just fell in love with them. I asked the man, "Did they have puppies?"

He said, "Yeah."

It was a struggle trying to raise money. I had to ask my whole family. My mom gave me 20. Daddy gave me 100. I was cleaning the car, cleaning the house, rubbing people's feet for three weeks and then I had the money. When I first got the dog, someone tried to steal her, but I came out and shot two in the air. When I walk my dog through the Eighth Ward, people reach for my dog, and I tell them, "Don't be touchin my dog. I don't want her to know you." They might offer me a thousand dollars to sell her, but I'm too attached to my dog even though she bites on everything from toy cars to people. That's why I gave her the name Shakie. Everything she bites, she shakes like she's trying to rip it a part.

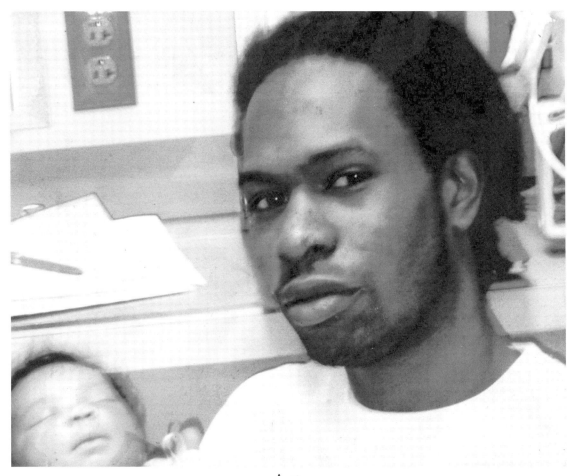

Brandon with Brandis Dugars, courtesy of the Russell family.

Brandis *Sister* Brandis Dugars

My mama popped up pregnant. My sister, Brandis Dugars, was born. I was saying to myself, "I can't believe this." I never thought my mama would have a girl.

The first night she came home my brothers and I could not stop looking at her. Brandon was there, too. When we tried to touch her hands, he slapped ours and said, "Don't touch her hands. Go wash yours."

When my sister made about a month, my mama started to let me hold her. On the rare occasion when I would watch the baby, she would say, "I'm about to go to the store, hold my baby. I'm coming right back" When she would leave, I would call her phone and say, "Ma, where you at?" She would say, "By Ne Ne house." I knew she'd be a long time—they always talk for hours. When she came back, I would give her the baby and run. She would say, "I wasn't gone long."

Making Clothes

Pernell wearing one of the outfits he designed, courtesy of the Russell family.

When I came home from Houston, I started buying paint and patches. I would buy Hollister and plain white v-necks from Walmart and have names of where I was from printed on them and paint over the stitching in the clothing. I would even paint or spray paint my shoes. Whatever would come to my mind, that's what I would do: skulls, stripes, even wards. Skeletons show where I'm from. It stands for Hard Head, which is what we call ourselves in the Seventh Ward and the St. Bernard Project.

When I did it, I switched into a different person. I was focused and wasn't worried about anything other than my designs. I lost track of time and would be up for hours. When I finished my work, you should have seen the reception I got from people. Some people were like, "Man, where'd you get that from?" When I said, "I made it," the first thing they said was, "How much would you charge me to make one?" I gave them my number and sometimes they actually called.

Skateboarding

I never thought I would be a skateboarder because I usually see white kids doing it. When I was younger I used to ride around the St. Bernard, and bust my ass. I really used to mess myself up. Maybe because I didn't have good balance. Now that I'm older, it's easy. I'm really good. I can do a kick flip and all kinds of tricks.

Now there's a gang of us riding around the Eighth Ward. People look amazed, like they never saw black kids skateboarding. People say, "Look at him, he wants to be white." They call me an "Oreo"—black on the outside and white in the middle.

We really ride our skateboards all over the city. You can catch us in the French Quarter just showing the white boys we can do it, too. We are better than some of them. When I skateboard by myself, I feel like I'm relieving stress. It's a way for me to think. At night, I go riding by myself. My mama would ask me what I'm doing, "I tell her, "Nothin. Just chillin." She would say, "Stop playing with me. Where you been?"

"Riding my skateboard."

She will say, "You should be white. You dress white, you even skateboard."

I said, "I'm me, man. I have my own swagger. You must want me to be like everybody else."

My mama says, "No, I just want what's best for you."

"I'm not like everybody else." I meet up with my friends and have a long day of riding to release all the madness my mom built up inside of me. By the time I got home, my legs are tired. Here comes my mom again, "You been riding that skateboard?" And I say, "I'm me."

Pernell skateboarding in the Eighth Ward, by Terrance "T-Tiga" Alford.

93

Interview with Stephen Fontenot, Co-Owner of Humidity Skate Shop

Stephen at Humidity, by Abram Himelstein.

I've been skateboarding for some time. One day, my teacher asked me to interview her friend Stephen. At first I didn't want to do it. When we got to his store in the French Quarter he was a little late. My first impression was, "This is gonna be boring. I don't want to do it." But when he opened the shop, it was pretty cool.

At the beginning of the interview, I thought Stephen was your average white guy. Never judge a book by its cover— he's white with flavor. Besides all that, I was so nervous, I was glad that Rachel was there. She pushed me to do the interview and once we started talking we were on the same page. He made me feel welcome and relaxed.

Pernell: So where did you grow up?

Stephen: I grew up originally in North Louisiana in a small town called Mansfield, outside of Shreveport.

Pernell: What was it like there?

Stephen: It was pretty quiet. Just a little small town. My dad worked for International Paper and my mom was a typical stay-at-home mom.

Pernell: How did you get involved in skating?

Stephen: Well, I felt very awkward growing up in the small town. I was kind of a shy kid—not typical in certain ways. At least for guys, there was a lot of pressure to be into football and baseball, and I wasn't

into it. I felt very alienated. It's so funny cause I used to be like, "Oh, I hate football." Well, now, I enjoy it. I'll watch football on a Sunday. When I was a kid, it would drive my dad nuts cause he wanted to watch the game with me and I'd be like, "Ah, dad, it's crap." My dad was a big outdoorsman, too. I used to fish with him. Hunting, not so much, because it required getting up at four a.m. and I'd be like, "No, I'm not about it." And then I used to be a stringent vegan and that caused a lot of strain on our relationship.

One day, I saw a skateboard magazine in the grocery store. I got pretty excited about it and decided that's what I wanted to try to do. There were no skate shops. You'd have to drive an hour to the bicycle shop that sold four boards in the back. A lot of it was mail order. For my very first board, I just kept begging my parents and they finally ordered it for my birthday.

Pernell: What was hard about it?

Stephen: Probably the hardest part first was figuring out the balance and getting into the routine. It's still hard every day, but it's so much fun at the same time.

Pernell: What did you like about it most?

Stephen: I didn't have to be around a lot of people. There was no team aspect involved. There were no coaches. I could just figure it out on my own and if I wanted to go in one direction for a week of trying certain tricks, I could do that and not have to worry about if it was right or wrong. As I got a little older, pushing around in the downtown area of my small town and then going to other towns and skating around, exploring other cities. That grew into another key interest, of traveling and exploring new things.

Pernell: How did you move to New Orleans?

Stephen: I graduated high school and then I got into University of New Orleans. I moved down here to study anthropology.

Pernell: What do you like about New Orleans?

Stephen: New Orleans? I mean, there's so much I like about it. The fact that everyone's so friendly. I like the tightness of the city. I use my skateboard a lot just in transportation. We used to live over on Spain Street and North Roman by the St. Roch Park before the storm.

Stephen skating in a swimming pool, by Todd Taylor (aka Uncle Fluffy).

Pernell: I live around there. What would you change?

Stephen: Honestly, in so many ways this city is anti-kid and anti-youth. I feel like it's so limited—the avenues of activity that kids can do, and trying to get something started has been just driving me nuts. I mean, it comes back to skateboarding. I would love there to be more skate-friendly stuff in the city.

Pernell: We all go to the skating rink or the teen clubs. We just don't want to stay home.

Stephen: That's what I mean. You don't want to stay

Stephen with Halloween skateboard, by Abram Himelstein.

home. When I grew up in Mansfield, dude, it was like that. You're just like, "What are we gonna do? What are we gonna do?" What can you do? You find a ruckus.

Pernell: What was the skateboard scene like here?

Stephen: Man, it has changed a lot. It's super cool, now. I just remember there would be points when you felt like, "Man, there's five dudes that skate in this city," and you go push around and you don't run into a single soul. In the past couple years, it seems like it's completely blowing up and there's more kids skating than ever.

And guys are doing their own little graphics—drawing on their boards and talking about trying to do t-shirts. That's something else I would love to be able to do—get kids working on t-shirt graphics and making their own little small little companies.

Pernell: I do that.

Stephen: You do? That's sick. Stuff like that is at the core of skating. Skating is not just pushing around and flipping your board around, but also how you look at stuff differently. That translates into so many-other things.

Pernell: I didn't bring my own designs, but I need help with them. Sometimes I will have no ideas.

Stephen: Right. Have you ever done them on t-shirts?

Pernell: Uh-huh.

Stephen: Yeah? A lot of times it's looking around at your environment and trying to get some influence that way. I'd really like to check out some of your stuff sometime.

Pernell: All right.

Stephen: And maybe we could do a shop shirt, you know. Like, if you come up with some cool graphic that you did we could do it as an artist shirt. That'd be something fun.

Pernell: Do you have problems with the police?

Stephen: In my experiences, honestly, I've never run into too much problems with the police in Orleans Parish for skateboarding. There has been two or three times when I've seriously been like, "Oh, man, we might just go to jail right now." But that's rare. When you're out skating downtown, you hardly ever run into problems with the police. It's more like private security and that's just like, "Hey, man! Get out of here!" But as I get older, I get a little more fearful of having to deal with the judicial system.

When you go out to Metairie or Kenner to try to skate, that's when it becomes a huge issue. The Vans Team was here two weekends ago—it's a pro shoe company—and Phillip was taking them around to some spots. They were out somewhere on the West Bank and the cops were totally freaking out on them—threatening to throw them in jail, threatening to shoot them. Pretty harsh stuff. It spooked those guys pretty bad to where they were wanting to get on the plane back to Cali the next day.

Pernell: If I'm walking down the street at night by myself, the police will often try to start something. If I'm on my skateboard, they'll think, "Oh, just a skateboard kid. He ain't got nothin. He's not about to do nothing."

Stephen: Right. Exactly. It's weird how you can change one little accessory and you're something else.

Pernell: When did you open the shop?

Stephen: We opened the shop in September of 1999.

Pernell: Why did you decide to open the shop?

Stephen: Well, basically the existing shop was going to go out of business. By that point, there was never longevity involved in the skate shops. Heidi and I decided we really wanted to do something solid—a cornerstone in more of a national sense where when

Heidi and Stephen when the shop first opened, courtesy of Stephen Fontenot and Heidi Goldman.

people would come to town, they would know about the shop and know to go there and it would be a representation of skateboarding in the city. That's why we opened it in the Quarter, so it would be easier for people from out of town to find us.

Pernell: Do you think skateboarding is just for white kids?

Stephen: Absolutely not. There's always been black skateboarders. There's always been Asian skateboarders. It's definitely not just for white kids. Before, it was so small and underground. The only exposure you got was from one or two magazines. If you were able to come across that magazine, then you might realize, "Oh, there's Ray Barbie," who was actually one of the guys who was down here from Vans. He was one of the legends and a black skateboarder. But you would never see it on T. V. because you would hardly even see skateboarders on T. V.

In the 80s, skateboarders were, "Rah! Punk rock!" That alienated a lot of people. Recently, it's been a lot more visible within the hip hop community with guys like Lupe. Currency's the big local guy that skates.

Pernell: Yeah, my cousin saw Currency do it and he started doing it, and then I picked it up from my cousin. Then, they had this one dude come around our neighborhoods and he's got a skateboard—now he's got everybody he knows on a skateboard.

Stephen: More and more, you're seeing skateboard companies owned by African-Americans and I think that's going to have a big impact. There's this one guy, Stevie Williams, just a phenomenal skateboarder from inner-city Philly and just came from nothing. Now he's got his own board company. He's got his own distribution. He was riding for Reebok.

We've had some kids say, "Yeah, I've always wanted to skate, but growing up, people would say that's a white boy thing."

Pernell: Right. Not all the people, just negative people will say something like that. I don't even pay them no mind. I just keep skateboarding.

Stephen: Yeah, man. That's it. People constantly yell crazy stuff.

Pernell: What kinds of people use your shop?

Stephen: All kinds. We used to just be a skate shop—just skateboarders would come in. But now, with the popularity of shoes, we'll be the only shop in the city that carries certain brands and there's more fashion-oriented people that come in.

Pernell: How do you work with teens?

Stephen: With teens? It works really well. Sometimes, guys can get a little rambunctious in the shop but, you know, that's cool. The shop has always been this balance between a clubhouse and a place of business. There's kids that come in all the time and hang out for a couple of hours in between skating or waiting to meet up to go skate. It's fun for me cause it keeps me grounded with everybody and it's fun for them cause everybody's hanging out, checking out magazines, talking about who's doing what tricks.

When we opened the shop, one of our main things was, "We gotta make sure it's inclusive to everyone." You walk into the shop and there's not gonna be anything about it that's gonna turn you off and make you think you shouldn't be there. We are just constantly are tryin to find ways to make sure kids can skate as much as they can and stay involved and stay positive.

Heidi and Steve

What's up ya'll me and
Aaron and Matt are in
dallas havin a blast. It
took us all day to
get here. we were talkin
about how Rad you
guys were and how
nice it was of you
to let us crash at your
place. If your ever
up NORTH you need to
stop by and hangout.
love Jon Aaron and Matt

THE NOCONA BOOT SERIES
The Scorpion

T-228

The Texas Postcard Co., P.O. Box 860708, Plano, TX 75086

Illustration courtesy of The Nocona Boot Co., Inc.

USA 20c
Harry S. Truman

19788 12345

POST CARD

Humidity Skate Shop
515 Dumaine St.
New Orleans, LA
70116

99

Shot of crowd at the Chat Room, by Aubrey Edwards.

PART III: CLIQUES

Pernell: Before Katrina, they had cliques. They just weren't as wild as they are now. They were in people's neighborhoods.

Daron: We had the Cut Boys in the Calliope.

Pernell: My cousin was a Cut Boy in our project. I can name a few of the other ones in the SBP—Dipset, State Prop, Young Gunnas, G-Block, the Valley Boys, the Baby Gunnas.

Daron: I heard of some of them. Cut Boys, the Porch Boys. The Little Mafia, the Valley Boys…

Pernell: Before Katrina, I was part of the BAC—Bad Ass Children.

Daron: [*Laughter*]

Pernell: Now there's all kinds of cliques—dancing cliques, people who've just been hanging together for a long time. Fashion cliques. Rap cliques. They don't have to be bad.

Daron: It depends on how you carry yourself.

Pernell: How your clique handles itself. If you dress preppy, you won't have a problem with the police.

FASHION

Pernell: You know back in the G, if you didn't have on G-Nikes you weren't nothing. Now, you can wear any kind of shoes you want.

Daron: Cliques will make sweaters and jackets. Representing!

Pernell: You want your clique to be known and I'll tell you who gets you known—girls! You talk to a lot of girls from everywhere. Girls talk, "I'm messing with this dude from Fresh Stars."

Daron: DJ D-Boi will get you known, too. He'll get up and give you a shout out, "Fresh Star! Fresh Star!"

DANCE

Pernell: I didn't know nothing about dancing in the project, son. Did you? You never saw dudes dancing in the project.

Daron: Not really.

Pernell: The girls are dancing and the guys would be—

Daron: Just standing there.

Pernell: They'd dance a little—they'd dip on a slow song.

Daron: Shuffle, move their shoulders. You could dance, but not shaking your booty and all that.

Pernell: If you were shaking, you were called a straight fag. The Blaza Boys, I could say, made it popular for guys to dance. But I don't care how much you dance, no dude is gonna listen to listen to bounce all day. It's dance music for parties and DJs.

Daron: People usually don't ride around and listen to bounce.

Pernell: The only time you'll catch us riding around listening to bounce is when we go by where beaucoup girls are at.

Daron: Because they'll dance on your car.

Pernell: I hate it when dudes who used to dance get around their people and go, "I didn't used to dance." I hate it when they do that. "Yeah, you used to dance, bra!" Those dudes are lying. I'll say it in front of anyone, boy. When I'm at school and people say, "He used to dance."

"I sure did."

Daron, by Lindsey Darnell.

Daron

Fresh Stars t-shirts, by Lindsey Darnell.

Fresh Star Clique

One day, this boy named Denzel who also went to John Mac came to fill out on application at Cane's. We ended up playing basketball at school a few days later and he told me he was hired. Gabby, Denzel, and I got really close and started hanging out together on the regular, going to parties and out to eat at Outback Steak House down the street from the mall after work.

One day, we were cleaning up and Gabby said, "Man, we need to make a clique." I'd never been in a clique before. It just sounded like a bunch of mess to me. At school and at parties, I overheard people beefing about their cliques. I was to myself. I didn't need all that. I had the studio. I wasn't looking for the group thing, but I really knew Gabby and Denzel and knew that if I was in a clique with them, they wouldn't create problems for us.

Denzel was down from the beginning, and they started throwing out names.

Gabby said, "It got to be something with fresh."

Denzel said, "What about the Fresh Stars?"

Fresh Stars sounded good to me, so that's what we stuck with.

I came home and told my dad, "I got a new clique, it's the Fresh Stars. You got to get down or lay down."

He said, "Man, you know I'm down with whatever."

I wanted him to be in the clique cause he's my dad but we act more like brothers to each other. And I have to say, the dude's fresh. I knew he would be good for throwing around fashion ideas and how to promote ourselves with t-shirts and sweaters.

The same week, Denzel and I were driving around with his cousin Markauise, this quiet but sneaky guy, in the backseat. We were in the front screaming "Fresh Stars! Fresh Stars!" to the Young Jeezy's, "I Put on for My City."

Markauise said, "What's a Fresh Star?" And we said,

"A nigga like us! That's our new clique."

Then we told him the same thing we told Chevy Earnhard, "You got to get down or lay down."

Markauise said, "I'm down for whatever."

Now we were five.

Markauise Frank

Markauise Frank wearing a Fresh Star hoodie, by Lea Downing

Before Markauise joined the Fresh Stars, we were cool, but not as cool as we are now. He never bothers anybody. That's why every time somebody tries to pick a fuss with him, I always jump in the middle of it. He is more laid back than anything. He grew up in the Sixth Ward off Rocheblave and Orleans in the Lafitte Public Housing Development. The youngest of three. His dad is from the Iberville, but he doesn't see him very much. When I asked him about it, he said, "My relationship with my mom is good because I stay with my mom but my relationship with my dad is like just off and on."

Although Markauise and Denzel are cousins, you would never know that because they have two totally different personalities. Denzel is the wild man. It seems like every time I call him, he's at a party, and he can never lie and say that he's somewhere else because of the loud music in the background. Sometimes he moves too much for me. We could be at one party and somebody would call him and tell him that it's popping at another party. With no hesitation, he would be like, "Y'all come on, we're about to dip to another party."

While Denzel is constantly moving, Markauise and I usually find a nice chilled spot and watch so that nothing happens to Denzel. Out of all of the Fresh Stars, to me Markauise is the coolest.

Daron: Where did you move when you came back home from staying in Texas?

Markauise: When I came back home I moved in the East off of Downman and Chef, on Shalimar Street. It's quiet, don't really have to be worrying about this and that person.

Daron: What is your definition of fresh?

Markauise: Dress to where you think you just fresh. If you think you fresh, then go ahead—you don't have to always be fresh to be a fresh person.

Daron: As far your clothes, what you like to wear?

Markauise: I like to wear Levi's, True Religions, MEK, USDA, and 8732. Sevens hoodies with our logo on it.

Daron: Have you ever been in any other clique beside the Fresh Stars?

Markauise: I have been in another clique. It was the Lova Boys. It was a dancing clique, but it didn't work out between us so we had to split. It was like certain people were saying, "This person is gay, that person—" Some of us were believing it so that didn't work out. Some still hang together, but some went their own ways.

Daron: All right, the clique name could have been anything. Why Fresh Stars?

Markauise: Cause we just like to be fresh and have nice cars and nice clothes.

Daron: Why do you like your clique only having a small number of people?

Markauise: Cause we don't have to have too much drama with other people.

Daron: How do you feel about having girls in the clique?

Markauise: It feels great because when we go out, people won't call us gay or whatever.

Daron: What's usually the reaction when the Fresh Stars walk through the door?

Markauise: It's like, "Oh they got a new clique out. Let's go see what they're about."

Daron: Do y'all get along?

Markauise: Yeah, we get along. It ain't that kind of clique. We're called the Fresh Stars. We like to dress.

Daron: Can you tell us one thing about each one of the Fresh Stars?

Markauise: Well, I'll start with my son, Money. You're the freshest of the clique. Now, Domonique, she's one of the ladies of the clique. She's well educated and we need that. I'm gonna do Fresh Star Denzel: He's a little wild. And we're off and on with Gabby. Roderick, he's the oldest out of the clique, so we have an older person to support us. Oh, and me, I'm just the quiet type— laid back. Just like to go and get fresh, talk to my lil partnas. Don't really be into too much stuff.

Daron: If you could change one thing about the clique what would it be?

Markauise: Well, we need to start hanging more together so people can know who we are.

Domonique Jacobs

Domonique and Daron, by Lea Downing.

Dom and I have known each other since my freshman year at John Mac. We talk to each other about everything from her boy problems to my rap career. Our moms are very cool——my sister and Dom both play for the volleyball team and they met watching the games.

Domonique is always changing up her style. One day she might have on True Religion jeans and a nice spaghetti strapped shirt, and the next day she might be wearing on a pair of pants with a button-down Polo shirt with MX shoes. After watching all of her fashion choices for a year strong, I decided she should be part of the Fresh Stars. I called all the members and ran it by them. They were cool with it.

It seems like Dom can detect when the Fresh Star boys are meeting up somewhere because every time we are together, she calls and asks what we are doing. One time me, Denzel, Markauise, and I were having a meeting about what we were going to wear for a party and in the middle of the conversation the phone rings.

Me: Hello?

Dom: What are we wearing to the party Friday?

Me: Ha ha.

Dom: What's so funny?

Me: We were just talking about that.

Dom: See, y'all always want to leave me out of stuff.

Me: It ain't even like that.

Dom: Uh huh, I bet. But any ways, I was thinking we should wear all black.

Me: You know what? That's a good idea.

Dom: I know, that's why I'm a Fresh Star. Ha ha.

Me: That's too crazy, but we are going to the mall tomorrow, so be ready around two.

Dom: Ok. I'm going to holla at y'all later. It's time to get my beauty rest.

Me: Ha ha. Iight.

I wanted to interview her to get her take on what it was like to join our clique.

Daron: You ready?

Dom: Yep.

Daron: Where were you born and raised?

Dom: I was born and raised in New Orleans, Louisiana in the Lower Ninth Ward.

Daron: How would you describe your neighborhood to someone who had never been there before?

Dom: Well, I'd describe my neighborhood as being fun and caring. Doesn't look too nice now but back then it was awesome. It was a great place to go and play.

Daron: Could you tell us about your parents?

Dom: I grew up in a single mother home by myself with three brothers and one sister. My mom worked for Sodexho and tried to do everything she could for us.

Daron: So for Katrina, did your family evacuate?

Dom: No, we didn't leave until after the levees broke and it was a mandatory evacuation. We tried to get everybody out.

Daron: And where did your family go?

Dom: To Baton Rouge, Louisiana by my cousin's family.

Daron: So how long did y'all stay in Baton Rouge?

Dom: A year. I lost everything so I was kind of depressed and didn't want to do anything.

Daron: And then when you came back to New Orleans where did you move to?

Dom: I was staying in the Lower Ninth Ward in a trailer. I live in Gentilly now. It's quiet, not too many people outside; don't know very many people. I don't care for it. We plan on going back to our old house once it gets rebuilt. No telling how long that will take at the rate it's going now, but we plan on going back.

Daron: What do you like to do in your free time?

Dom: I like to talk on the phone, go to the mall, play volleyball, twirl, and hang out with my friends.

Daron: Can you give us like a day out with your friends, like what would y'all do?

Dom: Well, if it was a group of girls, we'll try to go to breakfast. After we go to breakfast, get our nails or our hair done, go home, chill, watch movies, or go out to a party or a club.

Daron: How did you become interested in cosmetology?

Dom: When I was about 11, my mom stopped combing my hair so I had to comb my own hair. Doing hair is one of the ways you can make yourself look pretty. When I came to John Mac, I really didn't want to go to this school but I got interested in cosmetology. I fell in love with it so I just stayed here for the program.

Daron: The way that people talk about how bad John Mac is, is it really that bad?

Dom: No, it's really not that bad. We learn here. Well, I learn and the people who are in my classrooms learn. It's just like everything that happens at John Mac, they're so quick to put it on the news. Any other school, they keep it to themselves.

I don't like that we don't get to have dances. Everything is just work, work, work. We don't have anything to look forward to. There's nothing fun about coming here.

Maybe it's because the children don't do right, but I don't think everybody should have to suffer for it. I think we go to class enough to have events. They say every time we have something, something bad always happens, but I don't think that's true.

Daron: Which one of the Fresh Stars made you a Fresh Star?

Dom: You came to me one day in the gym and was like, "You want to be a Fresh Star?" I kept asking, "What is that? What is that?" You were like, "Man, if you don't know then you don't need to be in it. Man, it's our clique. We always be fresh and you got to rock the newest shoes. You got to be clean." I was like, "Well, that sounds like me. I can do that, that's easy."

Daron: Can you give us a day or a night with us being together?

Dom: All right. We'll be like, "Oh, I'm wearing some dark blue jeans, a pair of dunks, a nice shirt, jacket, and scarf." We all wear just about the same color. I liked when we all wore the color red. Then we'll all meet up at one person's house dressed to

kill—fire, fire—and plan out how we're gonna go roll up in a club or a party.

Daron: Do the boys that you conversate with or talk to, do they have to be fresh?

Dom: All the time. You can't be a bum. You can't still be living—well, you can live with your mama, but you can't depend on your mama. You need your own job, your own car. You can't be like, "Oh, I gotta go ask my mama for that," because that means if I have to ask you for something, you have to go ask your mama.

Daron: What goals do you have for yourself in the future?

Dom: I plan on going to college, hopefully study prelaw. If not, I hope to open up my own salon, work about two days out of the week.

Daron: Do you plan on staying in New Orleans?

Dom: No, not really. I really don't want to stay in New Orleans.

Daron: Why not?

Dom: It's not much to do down here. I think if I go somewhere else, I'll have more opportunities. I really want to experience somewhere else.

You can look for me in the future. Somewhere, I know I'm gonna be successful. And then I can remember, "Oh I remember my friend did the Neighborhood Story Project and I had an interview with him."

Getting Known

We started making a name for ourselves. At parties, we stayed together to make a bigger impact. The Party Crashers had come on the scene around the same time as we did, but they were more popular because there was more of them. When we'd see each other at parties, we'd dap each other off and dip through the crowd together. We felt famous.

I didn't have any problems with the Stars, but to be honest there are a couple of things that I was against. Gabby's every other day 1,000 dollar shopping sprees—I wasn't a fan of it because she had to work for that money, and by her not saving she won't have money put to the side if she falls off. Denzel sometimes can be too wild, which doesn't help him open his eyes to life. And they'll get mad at me because I don't feel like going out. My instincts just tell me I shouldn't sometimes. And my mama always says, "Follow your first mind."

After a year together, Domonique and Denzel graduated from John Mac. Both of them go to Delgado Community College. Gabby stopped working at Cane's about a year after we started the Fresh Stars. We don't see each other as much now that we aren't sharing shifts or a plate of hot wings at the Outback.

As a fashion clique, we have to keep making clothes with our logo on it to stay known. I started to feel like maybe we needed to do more—that there was more out there for us.

Pernell dancing and wearing clothes he made, by Melvin Russell.

Pernell

Crowd in the Chat Room, by Aubrey Edwards.

How I Learned to Dance

When I came back home from living in Houston, I started hanging out at the Chat Room. It's just a little teenage club on Tulane Avenue. Doors open at seven and it used to get over around 12. The DJs play bounce music. You take a regular R&B song and put an up-tempo beat on it or local rappers like J-Rock and Flipset Fred make their own songs. Some of my favorites tell you to "Move your body like a snake," "Watch your waist line," or "Rewind." They got all different kinds of dances and one night I stood on the edge of a circle that formed around this guy, J-Dog. He was jooking and dipping. I wished I could dance like that.

I went home and tried to do it. I was practicing in the living room to the song "Complicated" remixed with a bounce beat. My aunt Moonie tried to show me how to jook, but it was hard. I had never danced a day in my life, and worried that maybe I didn't have the rhythm.

aunt: Moonie

Soon after, they opened the Shake Box—that's on Claiborne and Pauger in the Seventh Ward. I started really getting into dance. I'd go almost every weekend to steal people's moves.

I was sad at first. I got burnt by T-Dog, who was part of the Dynasty Boys, and he wasn't even that good. I was dancing and he tapped me on my shoulder to challenge me. He started showing off his footwork and shoulder work. I froze up like a popsicle and everybody started laughing. I felt played and said to myself, "You looked like a dumbass." I never wanted it to happen again.

Dance Groups

There are all kinds of dance cliques and they change all the time. In the last few years, many have come and gone. Let me name a few of them: the Fly Guys, Crowd Movers, Take Ova Boys, Game Ova, Lova Boys, Blaza Boys, Double Time Boys—you get the picture. There are two different kinds of dancing—shoulder work and shaking. I learned to do both. It started to feel natural and I began getting noticed.

When I'd be on the dance floor, people would make a circle around me and Javae, who was known as known as Geek Kid Vae because he dressed preppy, geeky-like, with bow ties, collared shirts, and sweaters wrapped around his shoulders. I began to dress preppy, too, with clothes from American Eagle and American Apparel.

Jave invited me to be in a dance clique he was starting. He came by my house and told me, "It's gonna be me, you, Charlie, Butter, and Gee."

Me, you know I'm from the St. Bernard, while Javae, Butter, and Charlie are from the St. Thomas. Gee's from the Ninth Ward. Vae's the best one in the clique and Butter's a gangsta and a dancer at the same time. He doesn't let anybody play with him. Charlie's a clown. We'll be talking to some girl and Charlie would come out the blue and say, "Naw, Doo. The girl don't like you."

Vae was in charge of the clique and said, "We're gonna get paid if we do shows."

I said, "Shows?"

"We're gonna do shows at the skating rink."

"We're not gonna dance at the Chat Room? What about the Shake Box, or the new club, the Play House? Everybody be there."

Vae said, "Nigga, we just started. I'm working on a roll call."

Later, I was walking in the Eighth Ward and people were asking me if was I with the Geek Kids. They said, "I hear them dudes is the truth."

Outside the Chat Room, by Aubrey Edwards.

Javae Turner, by Lea Downing.

Interview with Javae Turner

I met Javae when my auntie wanted me to make him an outfit for his birthday party. I had only seen his face a few times in the project, but I made him a Hollister outfit with skulls and other designs, and he gave me an invite to his party. When I got there, Vae was dancing and I said, "Man, look at these niggas dancing." I thought it wasn't something I'd be into doing, but Vae had a lot of energy. After awhile, it started looking cool to me.

Since that night, we started hanging out. He does not like to stay inside. All he says is, "Let's go here, Let's go there." I mean, every teen club in the city should be rich off him. Youngin, the 50/50, the skating rink—just everywhere.

After he formed the GEEK KIDS we decided that name sounded childish so we changed it to Fly Guys. We kept that name for a little minute and then two other dance cliques merged—the Multi Guys and the Family Guys. They became MG2FG and we joined them, too.

119

Pernell: So where did you grow up?

Vae: I grew up in the St. Thomas Housing Development.

Pernell: What kind of music did you listen to growing up?

Vae: Mainly rap. Lil Wayne.

Pernell: What did your mama like to listen to?

Vae: Blues.

Pernell: Blues?

Vae: Yeah, a lot of old stuff.

Pernell: Did you grow up knowing Jubilee?

Vae: Yeah, yeah, I grew up knowing him.

Pernell: What was it like playing on his team?

Vae: Oh, it was fun. Had a lot of fun. Went to the championship, but we lost.

Pernell: What position did you play?

Vae: I played running back.

Pernell: Were you upset when the St. Thomas closed?

Vae: No, not really.

Pernell: Why weren't you upset?

Vae: Because I was ready to move anyway.

Pernell: Where did you move after it closed?

Vae: I moved to around the St. Bernard.

Pernell: How did you feel when you moved around the St. Bernard?

Vae: I was scared when I first moved around there. I never used to go outside. I just stayed inside.

Pernell: Tell me a story that you remember about being in the St. Bernard.

Vae: One day I was riding my bike. A dude named Shaq came and asked me if he could ride my bike and I let him ride it. He said he was going to the store. I stood right there and he never came back—he jacked my bike.

BOUNCE DANCING

Pernell: How long have you been dancing?

Vae: I've been dancing since I was little.

Pernell: Who are your favorite DJs?

Vae: DJ Show Boy, C.J., DJ C-Baby, and DJ Raspin Great.

Pernell: Is dance a big factor in your life?

Vae: Yeah, now it is.

Pernell: Why do you think it's a big factor?

Vae: Cause I like it, and it gives you like a lot of—

Pernell: Gets you known?

Vae: Yeah, it gets you known in the city.

Pernell: How does your family feel about your dancing?

Vae: They're cool with it.

Javae Turner, by Lea Downing

Pernell: My mom and my family support me, but not my dad. He doesn't like it. He thinks that's for gay people. And my friends who I grew up around, they are like, "You dancing, you shaking—that's for girls. That's for fags."

Vae: I know I'm not gay. If I dance in a club, I know when I get off the stage, beaucoup people are gonna start talking to me and coming up to me. That's money. You can make money from that.

Pernell: Ohhhh! I remember this one time I was talking to these girls and I tried to get one of their phone numbers. She told me, "I don't like boys that dance." And I was like, "Why?"

She's like, "If I go somewhere and he goes somewhere and both of us dance, I don't like that." What are the differences between the way girls and boys dance?

Vae: When boys dance there's more to it. When girls dance, they're just shaking—that's it. They just put their hands on the walls, but we do a lot of stuff.

121

GROUPS

Pernell: What was the first group you ever got in and how old were you?

Vae: The first group I ever been in was the Takeover Boys and I was like 12.

Pernell: How did you get in?

Vae: We used to hang with each other and one day they decided to make a group. I was with them that day, and they just asked me to be with em.

Pernell: What are some of your favorite groups?

Vae: Blaza Boys and MG2FG.

Pernell: How did MG2FG get together?

Vae: I was with the Takeover Boys and they have another group named the Rock Hard Boys. They used to hang together and one day they was just like, "We about to become a big ole group." First they named it Family Guys. Then, when we started hanging with my friend Dut, he was with Multi Guys and we was like we were going to put our two groups together and we just named Multi Guys to the Family Guys.

Pernell: I remember we was at the skating rink and everyone was shaking—I was the only one moving my shoulders. I felt so stupid because I didn't know how to dance. I just walked off and everybody was asking me why I wasn't dancing. I was like, "I ain't feel like it." I lied. I didn't really wanted to tell them I didn't know how. And then you came up to me and asked me why I'm not dancing, and I just looked at you stupid because you knew I didn't know how to do it.

Vae: I think that was on a Friday at a Shake Down.

Pernell: I came a long way from nothing. We used to be in the room and I was like, "Man, I ain't never gonna get it—I'm too skinny." You were like, "If Mario can do it, you can do it."

Vae: Yeah, you did come a long way.

BATTLES

Pernell: What is a battle?

Vae: When two people from two different groups dance against each other.

Pernell: How do you feel when everyone is watching you dance on stage?

Vae: I feel good. People go home and will ask us to start dancing for their parties and we get booked for shows.

Pernell: You're not nervous?

Vae: Nuh-uh. The first time I did it I was nervous, but I got used to it.

Pernell: Give me a number of people that you've battled.

Vae: I battled a lot. Probably more than a hundred people.

Pernell: That's a lot.

MOVES

Pernell: Who is your favorite dancer?

Vae: Blaza Boy Noonie—the way he dances, I've never seen it before.

Pernell: Tell me some of your favorite dance moves.

Vae: Swiggle, Iggy Pop.

Pernell: You might want to just describe them.

Vae: Swiggle is when you move your shoulders and move your body. Iggy Pop is when you keep spreading your legs on your toes and doing a lot of hand motions.

Pernell: What is a T-Lo and where does it come from?

Vae: Oh T-Lo, that comes from my big brother, Tyrone. It's like a crazy dance. He moves his arms back and forth. I remember one time I was in the Chat Room when I had to battle Black from the Blaza Boys and I won. I did the T-Lo—I brought it back out and made everybody go crazy in there. It hadn't been used in a long time.

Javae and Pernell, by Lea Downing.

How You Do That? *Uncle Melvin*

Even though he is younger than me, my uncle Melvin still tries to tell me what to do like he's the wiser one. We're together everyday. We always fuss but I got his back. He just has this mentality to be real. Melvin's a great football player. A lot of people who have watched him play respect him like he's a god or something. He's only a freshman at John Mac, but he starts on the team.

Like a lot of dudes, though, Melvin is conflicted about dancing. When I come around sometimes he'll say the way I dress looks gay, but when we're alone he tells me, "I want to dress like you." When I dance in public he makes fun of me and says, "Ya fag!" and start laughing. But when we get by ourselves he will say, "Show me how to do that."

Melvin dancing, by Pernell Russell.

Battle for My Name

It all started when there was a Bob Marley party at the Chat Room. I met up with some of my MG2FG fam. We were chilling, dipping to the beat with the Blaza boys. Once Sissy Nobby saw us all together, he started roll calling. He said, "Kunta and the Rasta himself, Dua Dua, let's go." Dua Dua started to swim and Kunta started going crazy. They're both MG2FG so it wasn't a real battle, just dancing.

Then Nobby called Boom and Monte, and the battles began. Boom, only ten years old, was too small so Dua Dua grabbed Vae, pulled him on the stage by his sweater, and told Nobby, "Call Vae." Vae and Monte started battling. Monte got on the ground so Vae started mixing and swiggling. On the floor, Monte didn't have many options so he just kept shaking and ended up losing the battle.

Next was Ike and Mario. When Nobby called their names everybody said, "Ohhhhhh!" Both of them are skinny so it seemed like a good match. Nobby said, "They look like stick people," and the whole crowd laughed. Mario had a serious look on his face like he was scared. Ike was dancing smooth and calm. Mario was going crazy, bringing out all his moves. He still lost.

Then Nobby called Kunta and L-Baby. Kunta got on the stage and was like, "I'm tired of burning L-Baby." When he said that, L-Baby started doing moves we had never seen him do before, like swiggling and mixing. When he snapped his head to the beat, his hat went from the stage all the way to the back of the Chat Room. So Kunta got for real, going hard. He was swimming and did a move where he ducked and it looked like he was diving under the water on beat. That did it. When the song stopped, Kunta was still dancing. He turned around and said, "Wait, I wasn't finished. That's it?!"

He's goofy like that. He said, "Come on, Doo." When I saw him tell Nobby to call my name, I tried to run, but Mino grabbed my hood and said, "Nobby, call Doo!"

I went up on stage and Nobby said, "Let me see who you can battle." Then out of the crowd Doo came. Well, the wanna-be Doo.

Nobby said, 'What's your name?"

"Doo."

"Well, it's a battle for your name!"

The beat started and I just started off swiggling, snapping, mixing, you name it. Doo was dancing so fast he looked like the fast forward of a tape. Then Nobby grabbed the wanna-be and said, "You're not ready for him!"

The crowd was like, "Ohhhhh!"

Nobby declared, "The real Doo, MG2FG!!"

Chat Room Pics

One day in class I was writing a story about the Blaza Boys and MG2FG and Rachel kept telling me, "I need pictures of y'all dancing."

On Valentine's Day, Rachel, eight months pregnant, Javae, and I met up with a rock-n-roll photographer named Aubrey and went to the Chat Room. Vae and I were paying our money and the owner kept asking Rachel and Aubrey, "Are you sure you want to go in?!"

When we got in, my focus went to the stage. I saw Vae calling Dua Dua as he battled Lova Boy Mario. Rachel and Aubrey said, "Let's go upstairs and take pictures." Everybody on the dance floor kept looking at us. Afterwards, we went to the back of the club and Kunta and Dua Dua start dancing first, then Vae and I started dancing and I slipped. No one saw it. We kept dipping back in the crowd and as we were talking, Aubrey was taking pictures.

Then I looked in the corner. I saw Vae battling one of the Pro Kids, then a Double Time boy, T-Rex. I didn't even know he shook—he used to just move his shoulders.

I looked over and saw Pat and Boom dance. Boom is about four foot six and Pat is average height for 16. Pat tried to fight Boom. Boom's big brother, who is about five foot one told Pat, "I'ma smash you."

Pat said, "You gonna smash me? I'll cave your heart into your body."

I thought about how I left my girlfriend inside on Valentine's Day. I was only supposed to stay an hour. I immediately told Rachel, "Bring me home."

When I got there all my girlfriend said was, "An hour, real!!! Your book is more important than me."

I couldn't say anything.

Owner of the Chat Room, by Aubrey Edwards.

Kunta, Money, Dua Dua, Vae, and Pernell (aka Doo) at the Chat Room, by Aubrey Edwards.

Both pages: Kunta and Dua Dua dancing, by Aubrey Edwards.

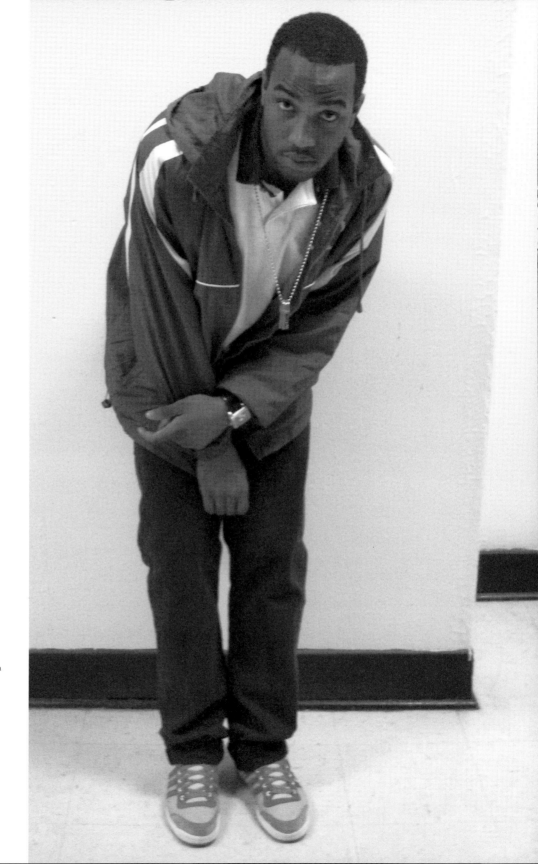

Dawan "DJ D-Boi" Gibson
Jordan, by Lea Downing.

Interview with Dawan "DJ D-Boi" Gibson Jordan

DJ D-Boi and I became friends through school and dance. I knew him in the project, but I didn't know him well. What can I say? He is one of the best DJs in the city. He's at every party and event, and is also one of the best dancers. He's been dancing for over ten years and is a legend in the game. Every bounce dancer looks up to him—even me. He is the head of the Party Crashers, a clique known for their dancing and DJing.

This interview at John Mac was my first time doing an interview at school talking about our outside life. I learned so many things. I never knew he had a daughter or so much on his mind.

Pernell: So where did you grow up?

D-Boi: I grew up in the St. Bernard on Milton Street. I forgot my address to the apartment I was living on, but I grew up in the project. [*Sounds of the John Mac band in the background*]

Pernell: What kind of music did you listen to growing up?

D-Boi: Oh, I listened to New Orleans traditional bounce music all day and a little rap music. Bounce was the favorite, though, because that's all I listen to and make beats for now.

Pernell: What were DJs like in the St. Bernard?

D-Boi: The DJs who I looked up to were the hottest back then.

Pernell: Jubilee?

D-Boi: Jubilee was one of them, but he's not from the St. Bernard. When I was in the project, we had Katey Redd, Big Freedia, Chev off the Ave and Vodka Redo just coming out with new songs, giving that vibe and best believe, your grandma, your auntie, all them were shaking out there when the punks came and performed live. That's who had the crowd rocking. And they still do.

I'm not gonna lie. If it wasn't for the punks, the bounce wouldn't be the way it is now. They've got to stop hating on these punks and give them their props. They make their daughters and mothers and sisters dance.

Pernell: Real.

D-Boi: I rock with the punks. I don't have beef with them. I don't care if real niggas see me dap a punk off. They'll be like, "Oh he's gay because he dappin them up." Or they'll say, "I don't even listen to that beat. I don't even listen to bounce music." The whole time they're tapping their feet to it.

Pernell: Punks made bouncing what it is, bra. Look at Nobby. They made it what it is. It's hot now. Who taught you how to dance?

D-Boi: Tell you the truth, the Body Rockers taught me everything I know. I stole moves from each one of them because they're family. Remember when Jubilee came out with, "Do the Jubilee"? That's when I learned to start dancing because my sister was doing it. The first move I learned was dancing like a girl—p-popping, shaking. Once I got the vision how to do it, I went home and practiced over and over in the mirror. Mama's like, "Turn the music down." and I'm like, "A couple more hours, Mom. Let me practice, me and my people."

When I first started going to the club at 12 years old, I was like, "Man, look at all these dudes! They really cold." And then one day, I was at the Chat Room. Everybody's getting on stage. I'm like, "Call me up there! Call me! Call D-Boi!" My crew was the BADs, Bad Ass Dancers For Life. I got on stage and said, "You know what? Give me somebody out the Blaza Boy clique." I'm not gonna lie, it was a hot group, too, the Blaza Boys.

When I get with people who I already know and used to hang with, I'll be like, "Y'all feel that beat? Ooo, that's that crowd right there—let's go! Everybody at one, two…"

And we'll all start shaking. After we leave the club, we'll go by my house in the East. I'll put the music on and start dancing. Everybody will just fall in place, shaking. This how you get cold. This is how you enjoy your weekend.

Pernell: How did you become a DJ?

D-Boi: I became a DJ after Katrina when John Mac had their first talent show and 10th Ward Buck and DJ Lucky came to do an assembly. I hooked up with Lucky and he started to teach me. But I had been wanting to DJ because it ran through my grandpa's family. He and his brother did it, then my daddy did it, and I was like, "You know what, it's time for me to move out of here, get my own equipment, and start scratching and doing stuff on my own." My mom came and did a big party for me. I appreciate my mama for that.

Pernell: How did you get your name DJ D-Boi?

D-Boi: I got my name because I know the type of music people like. I know how a crowd shakes because I used to be a dancer. If you're a dancer, you know the vibe for people dancing in the street and the clubs out here. All they want is the beat. All you hear in the clubs is, "Put that beat back on, run it DJ." They hear the beat first and the lyrics later. The lyrics aren't too much, but that beat just comes in

DJ D-Boi at a birthday party in the Sixth Ward, by Pernell Russell.

with all type of samples from keyboards and drums and tenors.

Pernell: How did it feel when you are DJing and you see everybody dancing?

D-Boi: I like when they dance to my music—especially to the beat that I made with Flipset Fred, my artist, who made "Watch dat Waistline." They have all types of programs for making beats, but the one I use is Acid 4.0. My little homey DJ Tank came and put the program on my computer for me and taught me. You got mids, highs, bass to make a beat.

It was hard at first because the first thing you gotta learn is beat mapping, and beat mapping takes time. If you're a beginner, you'll be on it for hours trying to beat map it over and over until you get it right. I found out you have to count with it—how fast the beat is supposed to be: 1, 2, 3, 4 or 2, 2, 3, 4 or 3, 3, 3, 4. If you don't know how to beat map, it makes no sense to put a roll call beat with a Kanye West song. With that process, I came a long way, too. I watch and learn and steal from people how they do this and that. I like it.

Pernell: Have you ever seen the music change over time?

D-Boi: Yeah, it change over time because back then we used to have Triggerman beat and now we just have roll call beats. The tempo on a roll call beat is fast—108—and that's all people really shake to. Then you'll get a little Brown beat every blue moon, but the music has changed. Just like Sissy Nobby. Back then in 2002, Nobby was coming out with poosongs, and now Nobby's the hottest thing on that radio, just like Flipset Fred.

I give people chances. People say, "Okay, when you gonna do our roll call beat?" I don't rap, so I'm go tell you again: "Whenever Flipset Fred get ready, and y'all get your money together, we'll do y'all a roll call."

Pernell: How much do you charge for a roll call?

D-Boi: It's up to Fred, you know what I'm say?

Pernell: I got to talk to him.

D-Boi: Fred will charge you 20 dollars a name. People act like that was hard. Y'all gonna pay Nobby 20 dollars a name cause Sissy Nobby and Chev off the Ave the only ones who really make roll calls, but Chev off the Ave is no longer in the music business. That man's retired and lives out of town. Nobby's making roll call beats now. Flipset Fred is making the roll call beats.

Flipset Fred, by Aubrey Edwards.

Pernell: How often do you DJ?

D-Boi: I DJ every week. DJ 7 put me on with the Grinding DJs. I appreciate him doing that for me cause that's a step right there—now I can move up to more clubs or find a permanent club where I can DJ for older folks—18 and older—instead of for the teenagers because I don't want to be doing the teenagers all day. I want to do all the sexy things too.

For an older club, I'd play more R&B and less bounce. I want to change it up and have it rocking. I'd play bounce when I feel like they want the beat. "Who bout their money outchere? Where my independent ladies at?"

Then I'll go back for my fellas. They want to hear that real gangsta music, too. Then I'll just play something for my women and my men to get along and start dancing together, grinding on each other. That's when the R&B will kick in. I want to see them rocking, calling out my name. When they see me in the street, I want them to say, "What's happening D-Boi?" I want them to request me on 102.9, Q93, and all that.

Pernell: How much do you charge to DJ and for how many hours?

D-Boi: For four hours I charge 200 dollars.

Pernell: That's good.

D-Boi: If you just get the DJ it's 200 dollars but if you get the package deal, for me and Flipset Fred it's 400 dollars, you see what I'm saying? I also got a contract too for doing schools and shows out of town and stuff like that. Yeah, the prices go up for out of town and stuff like that.

Pernell: What are some of the clubs you DJ in?

D-Boi: I did the Chat Room, Club 50/50, Club Youngin, and the Shake Box.

Pernell: What are some of the ones you like the most?

D-Boi: The one I like the most is Club Youngin because that's the club that gave me the vibe I really liked. The girls shook all night to my beat. My speakers ain't no joke. My equipment is exclusive.

I also DJ after second lines. I like it uptown on Seventh Street because they don't just stand around on the sidewalk looking at you. They really get in the middle of the street and start bending over, shaking and clapping.

Pernell: Do you ever think you will stop dancing or DJing?

D-Boi: I don't think I'll ever completely stop dancing because of that vibe and that beat. I'm gonna move and do something for the crowd. They might be like, "Oh, I wasn't expecting D-Boi to shake like that. Ohhhh, I thought D-Boi retired." I'll still play around to show I still got it in me.

Pernell: What about DJing?

D-Boi: DJing, I just started. I'm not gonna stop until I'm 68 years old. I'm gonna keep going with this as long as we live. If I get rich off of being a chef, I'm still gonna DJ.

Pernell: What are some of the other things you do besides DJ?

D-Boi: I cook, I go to culinary school for that right here at John Mac. I learned from my mama and grandma in the kitchen, just watching them make rum and crumb cakes from scratch. I love to cook gumbo, but I'm into the baking right now. I bake all day—cheesecake, pecan pie, pralines, 7-Up cake.

Pernell: What are some of your goals?

D-Boi: My goal right now is to graduate from high school, go to college, become a chef, and then get my own business as a chef. I'm raising my daughter, too. She was just born on August 14, 2008. Her name Da'mari Jordan Gibson. She's a gorgeous little thing. I have a picture in my phone so you can see her—she right here.

Bull-dozed St. Bernard Public Housing Development, by Pernell Russell.

PART IV: PROTECTION

Pernell: Katrina made everybody grow up fast, fast.

Daron: They went to thinking that if they tore down the projects, the violence was going to go away.

Pernell: In some ways, it made it worse. You're beefing with somebody from another project and now you live down the street from them. And after the storm, it was easy to get your hands on a gun. Fifty dollars and you got a gun.

Daron: A lot of people found guns in houses.

Pernell: Sometimes I get that bad vibe—like, "Man, I ain't feeling this." You can tell when somebody's got a gun. They'll be holding their hip, walking fast. They want you to tell them something just so they can shoot you and get some stripes! People shoot people for nothing! "Oh, yeah, man! I just whacked him!" You didn't even *know* him. You did him something for nothing!

Daron: That's why you'll never see anybody go somewhere by themselves.

Pernell: I say you need about four people.

Daron: When somebody says, "light," you know what time of day it is.

Pernell: It's time to maneuver. As soon as you get outside: *Pow pow pow pow!* For nothing, cause you stepped on their shoe. One day Vae and I went to the Chat Room. It was a good ten of us and we're on the side street and this dude rolled up on his bike with his gun in his hand, just booting up. I had never seen this dude in my life.

GUN OR NO GUN

Pernell: You don't feel safe?

Daron: Not at all.

Pernell: When I'm around people from the project, I feel safe. When I was at the McDonogh 35 and Carver game, they were shooting. My little partnas out of the project came with their guns out and asked me, "You straight?" I told them, "I'm good."

Daron: I feel like gun or no gun, I still don't feel safe. Why you got one on you? You're not feeling safe.

Pernell: Protection!

Daron: It's a lose/lose situation.

Pernell: When you have a gun you feel like, "All right, I have a little something to protect myself."

Daron: But for how long? All I've got is street smarts and my hands. So many young people want to be gangstas. They feel like they have something to prove, like they want to make a name for themselves and thugging is the only way to do it. But I bet you got people who claim to be gangstas, but are really be inside writing.

Markauise, Daron, and Denzel at the studio, by Lea Downing.

Daron

Stuck in a Box

At times, it feels like I'm stuck in a box and there's no one that can help get me out. The harder I try to kick my way out of this box, my heart beats faster, my head starts to pound, and it feels like my stomach is in my back. I think about what makes me feel like this, and all I come up with is the fact that my uncle is in jail for a crime that he didn't commit.

uncle in jail

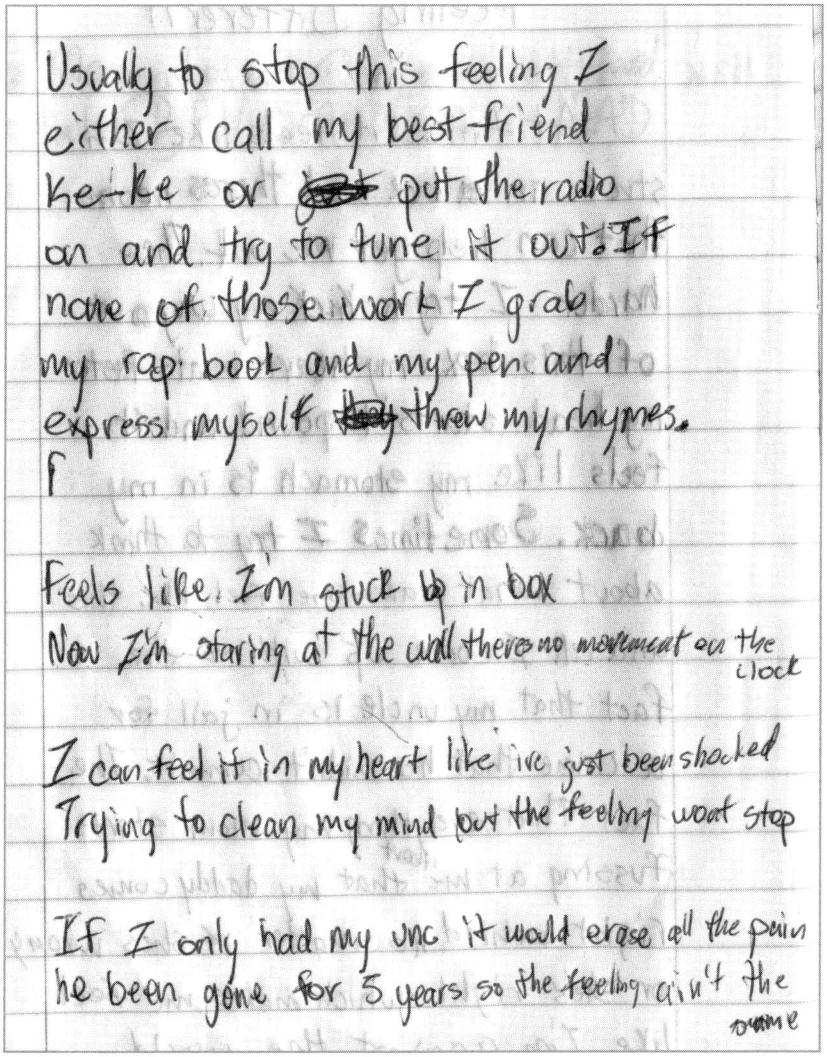

Usually to stop this feeling I
either call my best-friend
ke-ke or ~~put~~ put the radio
on and try to tune it out. If
none of those work I grab
my rap book and my pen and
express myself ~~thew~~ threw my rhymes.

Feels like I'm stuck up in box
Now I'm staring at the wall there no movement on the clock

I can feel it in my heart like ive just been shocked
Trying to clean my mind but the feeling wont stop

If I only had my unc it would erase all the pain
he been gone for 5 years so the feeling ain't the same

142

Every second every minute that goes by
If I didn't see have a the things I saw would it be me that
the story told
by.

When I'm in church it's my hands that I hold by
Unc always said fear nothing exspecailly no guy

So thats the madiet I go ~~easy~~ by
And its always me that these stories are wrote by

Dear Derry,

Wats up big dog? I know that its been a lil minute since I wrote you and . I'm sorry about that. I really have been thinking about you alot. Tooti made a song about them things you have been threw and all I do is play that song over and over. Even tho you are the one thats locked up it feels like I'm doing the time to. Man the city ain't the same anymore people gettin killed back to back. 2 of my lil dogs from the project got killed 3 weeks apart from each other. I try not to think about it so much cause it hurts me inside knowing that I use to be around these dudes everyday. I know now that they are gone they are in a better place but its still fucked up I go to the studio every chance that I get because thats one of the ways I express myself and release my anger. I'm really a dog at rapping now and by the time you come home we gone be gettin it and I'm gone be waiting outside of those gates with

a whip and 3 dime pieces for you. You might
that its funny but Im serious. I have been
working alot tryin to stack my money. Its
a tripp out here everybody want to be
gangsters now but you can see it in a
Nigga if they real or not. Well thats
enough about me write me back soon
I want to hear wats been going on. Stay
strong and keep in touch hope to see you
soon.

Love you
Always money

p.s heres a lil taste of wat I be spittin.

Na Im Gone - Save that

For the Next time. Be

Cool and keep ya head up.

LOVE YOU !!!!!

Drive to Hunts

Uncle: Derry Crawford

I wanted to do an interview with Derry, but he was locked up, getting it done was going to be a hard job. We thought about trying to get a collect phone call recorded, but Abram came up with the idea of taking the ride to Hunts to interview him. He tried to figure out how we could get in with a recorder, calling the warden and checking the web site. There were no easy answers, so we decided to just ride up there one Saturday morning. Abram stopped at my house to pick me up at eight o'clock.

AUNT

On our way to get on the bridge, my aunt Shanel called and asked if she could come along for the ride. Abram and I stopped and picked up her and her son, Elton. *(Son)* Once we made it to the entrance gate, we started to prepare ourselves, putting our cell phones away in the glove compartment, and putting lotion on our faces to make sure we weren't ashy. We hadn't seen Derry in six months and he didn't know we were coming.

We walked to Visitors' Center to check in, where there were 20 other families waiting to see their loved ones. There was a lot of tension on everyone's faces. Shanel, Abram, and I passed our IDs over to the guards, and told them we were here to see Derry Crawford. We knew Abram would probably be denied, but he wanted to try anyway, and sure enough they called his name, and told him wasn't going to be able to see my uncle because he hadn't had the security check.

We didn't know what the rules were about doing an interview—whether you had to have special permission. Our plan was to just have Abram take notes while I asked the questions, but now the interview looked more in doubt. I thought about smuggling in the recorder, but Abram convinced me it wasn't worth the risk of not being able to see him at all.

We were standing around for 15 minutes when they told us to line up. The lady guards searched the women, and the bus driver searched the men. He told us to look away from him while he was searching us and said, "It creeps me out to have men looking at me while I am touching their junk."

As we got on the bus, Abram went back to his car to wait in the parking lot. We rode to the visiting area. Beaucoup young people were lined up like they were in boot camp. We waited for my uncle in the cafeteria. I was excited to see him. He came in from the jail, and had to get searched, but didn't have to wear shackles. He said, "I didn't even much know y'all was coming!" I gave him a dap and a big hug. He looked good, wearing a pair of blue jeans and a blue shirt.

"What's up, dog? Man, I miss you."

We talked about how I've been working at Cane's, on my book, and rapping on the weekends. He said that he has been trying to learn carpentry so he can have a trade when he comes out. He said, "Man, I'm ready to come home!!" I wanted Shanel and him to have some time to talk, so I brought Elton to the concession stand. We came back with lunch, and I told him, "My book is missing your interview. I really need one with you."

1. Where were you born and raised?

2. What was your childhood like?

3. Where are your parents from?

4. When did they move to the Calliope?

5. Who took care of you?

6. Why did you begin selling drugs?

7. Who helped or showed you how to sell drugs?

8. What was your school experience like?

9. What are you feelings about guns—and have you ever owned a gun?

10. Did you ever have to use a gun?

11. Have you ever been shot or shot at? (Follow up and get story if he wants to tell it.)

12. How did you feel about living in the projects?

13. What age were you when you first saw a jail cell?

14. How many times have you been to jail?

15. How did you feel the first time you had to stand in front of a judge?

16. What was the longest time you have ever been sentenced to?

17. Before you started selling drugs, what did you want to be when you grew up?

18. Where do you see yourself ten years from now?

19. How do you feel about your family?

20. What are your plans after you get out of jail?

21. Do you think you are ready to get out of jail?

22. Do you regret anything you have done?

23. What is it you would do different if you got a second chance to start over?

24. How do you spend your time in jail?

25. Do you think selling drugs is wrong?

26. What advice do you have for me about the choices I can make?

27. Do you think guns make us safer?

28. What was it like to be in jail during Hurricane Katrina?

29. What are your feelings about New Orleans as a place to live?

He asked me, "Man, what's the book about? Why do you need an interview?"

"You got a major role in my book, and I need your own words to help the book be a success." I pulled out the list of questions and showed it to him: He said, "Damn, I got to answer all these questions right now? Can I write the answers out and mail them to you?" I guess it was a lot to talk about and I hadn't prepared him for it. I told him I loved him and reminded him how important the interview was. I didn't need to worry. I got a call from my aunt three days later telling me that the letter had arrived.

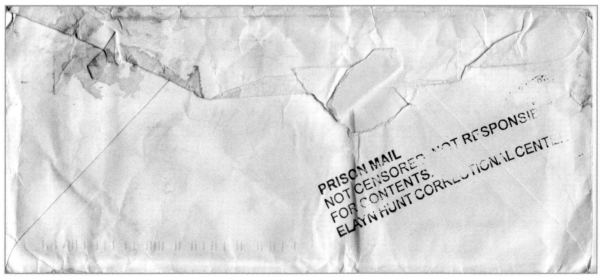

① I was born and raised in N.O. La.

② My childhood was fun my Mother bought me pratically everything I ever wanted

③ My father lives in Virginia and my Mother stays in N.O.La.

④ I was born and raised in the Calliope project up until I was about 14 years old

⑤ My Mother and my father took care of me until I started Hustling.

⑥ I Began to sell drugs at the age of 13, most of my friends was selling drugs I ~~not~~ wanted fit in and also because I wanted more expansive clothes and tennis shoes I wanted to be the flyest dude in school

⑦ My friends helped me sell drugs in the begining And when my ~~father~~ Mother found out I was hustling she started teaching me a little bit about selling drugs.

⑧ My school experience was nice I **use** to like going to school because I wanted too show off my new Kicks and clothes I Breezed straight through Elementary when I made to Junior high 7th grade thats when I knew I had a addiction for fast Money

9. I've owned plenty guns when you're living the Street life thats like mandatory

10. Yes

11. yes, I've shot at people and also I've been shot at.

12. Well, actually we lived kind of comfortable in the project So living in the project never was a problem for me

13. I was like 16 years old when I first went to ~~juvenile~~ juvenile gail

14. May be about twenty

15. The first time I stood in front a judge I actually thought it was cool.

16. The longest time I ever have been sentenced to is 8 years I am currently doing the sentence now

17. I wanted to be a football player when I was ~~growing~~ growing up

18. Ten years from now I plan to own my own house, Business, and hopefully I'll have two kids

19. I love my family besides their all I got

20. I plan to get a job hopefully offshore make some money and move forward with my life

21. yes. In fact this have been an life time experience for me.

22. no ⟶

(23) I probably would go through school and and get an Education I believe Knowledge is the key to success

(24) For me jail is like a College I spend my time wisely I like to read books mostly Educational books I'm always seeking knowledge I like to exercise daily

(25) yes I think selling drugs are for ~~numates~~ a complete waste of someones life

(26) I advise you to stay in school always strive to further your education never give up on life you can be anything you wanna be in life. Never sell drugs never carry a gun stay out of the street life because they got people in life counting on you to come to prison so that they can make a living and they have no problem sending you here for the rest of your life

(27) Do to the corruption and Violence New Orleans is not some where I would wanna live anymore.

151

Everybody Had Talent

My dad has been talking to my uncle about getting involved in Beat Box when he gets out of jail. I feel like I have a place in the business, too, but I also want to make a name for myself. When we moved back to New Orleans, John Mac had a much different rap scene. Everybody had talent. I was selling the Chevy Boyzs CD, but not many people had heard it around school. One day I was sitting in class and this dude named Kendrick came up with one of my CDs and a CD player. After he listened to it, he said that he didn't like it and that I was garbage. I told him that I could beat him in anything he did, and he replied by saying, "Not rapping." The class laughed and screamed, "Battle, battle, battle!" I said, "It's whatever with me."

The look in his eyes showed a big surprise at the word "battle" even being brought up. The way that all the kids formed a circle around one table reminded me of the movie "Brown Sugar," where all the old school rappers such as Slick Rick, Rakim, and Eric B. would meet in the park and form a freestyle circle.

Kendrick told his lil dog to run the beat with a pencil. He started tapping and Kennedrick told me to go. I was already mad at the fact that he had the class laughing at me. I gave him my hardest:

Never hesitate, give me the cash when I ask for it
Cause I won't hesitate to leave ya brains on the dashboard.

The class jumped up and down. Then Kendrick went. He seemed nervous cause he slipped in the middle of his verse. I didn't give him any time to recover. I went straight for the kill and rapped about everything he had on. The class was roaring with laughter.

I made a name for myself and his career had ended just like that. I didn't feel bad about it either. Everyone loses a battle, I just haven't met my match yet.

Denzel Abram, by Lindsey Darnell.

Interview with Denzel Abram

Back in the days when Denzel worked at Cane's he used to beat on the deep freezer while everyone listened to me rap. It made the shifts go by faster. He told me that he rapped, too, but I always took it like he gave it to me—as a joke—until one day he told me he wanted to come to the studio.

Anybody who wanted to come with me had to go through my dad first because he is so good at reading people. If he knew you were about bullshit or felt you would set us up (come back and steal our equipment) it was a no. He knew Denzel was an important part of the Fresh Stars, but the studio was sacred space so he asked, "You sure he ain't fake?" With confidence, I said, "Yes."

"It's cool, bra."

I called Denzel and invited him to come with me on Friday night. I didn't know what to expect cause a lot of people say they know how to rap but when they get behind the mic, they freeze up.

I put on one of my favorite beats by T-Sibley, a hard, punchy, hype beat, and told Denzel to write to it. After he finished, I told him, "Step into the booth and spit that shit." I was nervous because if he was garbage that would fall back on me.

When he started, I said to myself, "Money, his voice just sounds perfect on the track." He had a smooth, low pitch that you could never get tired of listening to. At the end of his rap he said, "Fresh Stars." My dad and T-Sibley looked more surprised than I was and Chevy Earnhard pitched the idea of making it a rap group.

We looked at each other and smiled. Denzel said, "I'm down for whatever."

But he didn't come to the studio very often. I got worried that he wasn't serious about being part of the team. On Fridays night, I'd call him and say we were on our way to the studio and he'd say, "Man....I'm doing something now. I'll call you back in an hour." He'd never call back.

I was still at Cane's and the music was a way out. During my shifts, all I could think about was music. The beep from the headphones and the sound of cash register opening made me think of beats. One day I was over at Denzel's house. We were on MySpace listening to somebody rap, and I tried to talk to him about it one more time. "This is where the money at and the rest of the bullshit will always be there." He seemed shocked. You could tell that nobody had ever gotten that serious with him like that.

A few days later, the phone rang. It was Denzel saying, "Son, son, I was thinking about what you was telling me and I'm ready to do this." I didn't take him seriously until he started calling on the daily asking about the studio. Once I saw that he was serious, we started going every day I didn't have to work.

Daron: Where were you born and raised?

Denzel: Seventh Ward, New Orleans. Back-a-town.

Daron: How is your relationship with ya mom and dad?

Denzel: Well, I only see my mom two days a week because she's a flight attendant, but we have a close relationship. She's the only person I have. My dad is dead.

Daron: How did you take it when you were old enough to realize that you didn't have a father?

Denzel: When I was young, I wanted to go out and do something stupid because my dad got killed, but as I got older, I figured out that was stupid. I miss him, but you have to move on.

Daron: How old were you when you found your love for music?

Denzel: I was around 14 years old and started listening to Nas, Lil Wayne, and Jay-Z, and tried to rap like them. A long time ago being at teen summit looking at Lil Wayne and looking at Fresh when the Hot Boyz were together—when they was a real clique—I wanted to be like them.

Daron: And did you have other people that influenced you to start rapping or it was just something that you wanted to do?

Denzel: Around then, I started having a lot on my mind, and started writing.

Daron: Basically you use rap to tell people what you were going through—like expressing your feelings?

Denzel: Yeah, I expressed my feelings through rap. I started putting them into my songs.

Daron: Are you using music as a getaway plan for money, or it's just something that you really love doing?

Denzel: Basically, it's not really about the money. It's just something I like doing to hopefully send a positive message to younger kids.

Daron: Dealing with all the rivalries between the hoods, how do you handle dealing with each other?

Denzel: It's not like because we come from different hoods, if they're beefing, we're going to have problems. We've been knowing each other for a long time now. We don't beef over nothing stupid like that. We're a group, we stick together.

Daron: So how do you deal with being around all this violence? Like, not being involved in all the violence?

Denzel: I just try to go to the studio instead of being out in the streets doing something stupid. I could be in the studio getting clean money.

Daron: So do you feel like your rap clique is good enough to make it?

Denzel: It's possible. Everybody has strong ideas. When they get on the track with us, it's hot. I like to get other people ideas. And Chevy Earnhard, he's older so I look up to him like the father I never had.

Interview with Markauise Frank, Part II

Markauise came with us to the studio all the time, but didn't rap. He liked listening to the music, and would sit on the couch and hype us up. When we were in the booth, he'd yell through the window, "Yeah, son, yeah! Run that shit!" He was familiar with the studio scene because his cousin is Mannie Fresh, one of the best producers to ever come out of New Orleans. He got his start with Cash Money and now works with all types of artists.

One day, we were sitting in the studio and Markauise was talking about a rap battle on YouTube. In the battle a man lost so bad that his friends who were with him hung their heads down and laughed.

I told him, "They ain't gonna kill me like that."

My dad said, "Man, you better stop battling before you slip up." He made me think about it. I've seen lots of battles where people take out their cell phones and record it. Once the image ran through my head it was no more rap battles for Money.

It was difficult. I watched a lot of rap battles and wanted to be in one so bad, but instead I had to focus on studying their raps and telling myself if I got in the ring, I'd have to be prepared for the worst. Many have lost respect lyric-wise. I had a rep to keep, so I stayed away from the battles and showed more aggression in the booth.

Markauise would tell us stories about how B.G. and them used to be in there rapping. It wasn't long before Chevy-Earnhard pitched another idea: "Man, y'all might as well start your own record label. Freshstar Ent." He brought us to a company meeting with lawyers who showed us the business and legal side of the rap game. Markauise said, "Man, it's a lot on our plate, but mark my words, it's going to be done."

Markauise, by Lindsey Darnell.

Young Zel, Money, and Keedy (aka Denzel, Daron, and Markauise, by Lindsey Darnell.

Daron: Can you tell us one of your goals?

Markauise: Well, that's to produce music and promote my Fresh Stars. I go to the studio every now and then to look at the people who do the producing. I like DJ Cally because he produces a lot of people's music. Mannie Fresh—he's my cousin so I want to work with him. Swiss Beats and DJ Pro-style—I like how they do their music. I want to be up top with them.

Daron: It's going to be Chevy Earnhard and Batman doing the production.

Markauise: My cousin and all them had a girl who was calling them different superheroes. They gave me the name Batman. Ever since then, I've been calling myself Batman. Sometimes I call myself Markauise. My family calls me Keedy. I had that name to start off with and I like that.

Daron: This is gonna be the year we really bring it out. We gonna have Fresh Star gear.

Markauise: We gonna have logos and all that.

Daron: Anything else you want to say?

Markauise: I just want to send a shout out to the Fresh Stars. Markauise, better known as Keedy or Batman. I'm just chilling here laid back doing this interview. There's a lot of stuff I've been wanting to achieve so if y'all listening, y'all can help me achieve my goals. I also want to be a movie producer and a book writer. I want to be all kinds of people. I want to be famous to help my family.

Daron: Be on the lookout for Fresh Stars.

Markauise: We comin.

Studio Sessions

On Friday, everybody meets up at the studio. The session will start around eight. T-Sibley is always the first one in and the last one out because it's his house. The Fresh Stars roll in on time followed by Chevy Earnhard a half an hour later. Special guests like Flee or Profit roll in after that.

The beginning of the sessions usually starts off slow. Once T-Sibley puts a beat on, everybody tries to come up with an idea for the song. I sit back on the sofa in my own world and watch the smoke from the rolled cigars come from both ends of the room. Once somebody comes up with a hook for the song, everybody wants to be on a songwriter's 16 bars. After we are done writing, whoever wants to be first on the song goes into the booth and lays their verse down. After the first person, it gets easier because you know what to come with next in your verse.

When everyone finishes, T-Sibley takes over, and mixes it down, smoothing out our voices and making the tracks come together.

Each time I begin to write, it sends me back in time when I used to watch my uncle try to write. I start wishing he was home, and imagine him sitting on the sofa writing with me. I know he says New Orleans isn't where he wants to be, so I try my hardest to be my best on every verse and make it in the rap game. From there, we'll be on our way to Japan, or anywhere else, if we want to.

T-Sibley at the studio, by Lea Downing.

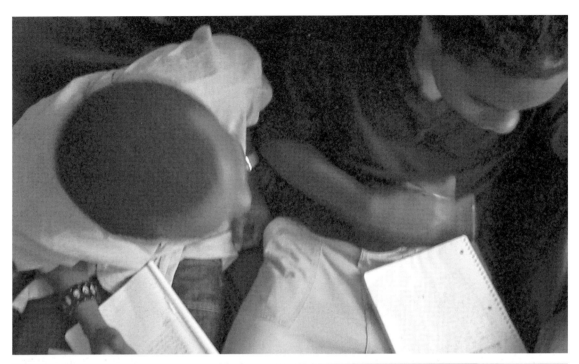

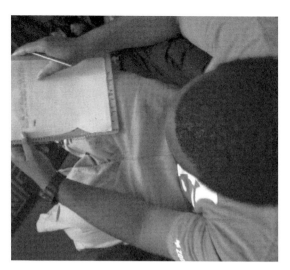

Previous Spreads: Working on lyrics at the studio. *Above:* The booth at T-Sibley's house: Flee, Denzell, Roderick, and Daron. Photographs by Lea Downing.

Fresh Stars Rap Clique: Chevy Earnhard, Money, Young Zel, and Keedy
(aka Roderick, Daron, Denzel, and
Markauise), by Lindsey Darnell.

Pernell his senior year of high school, by Rachel Breunlin.

Pernell

Homage to Brandon

I was by my daddy's house. My auntie called and said, "Bee dead." I said, "Man, stop playing." She kept calling me and so I was like, "Dad, bring me home." He said, "What for?" I said, "Bee got killed." He took me back across the river to Franklin

I got home and my mama was laying in the bed, holding my sister saying, "I can't believe that"—which became something she said every, every day. I didn't feel anything right then. When I saw everybody getting t-shirts made, I started to feel it.

When I woke up the morning of Bee's funeral, I was moving very slow. I did not even want to get out the bed, to tell you the truth, cause I didn't get any sleep. I was thinking about all the memories of us from the project, the way he used to take care of me and my brothers in Texas, how he never left us when we came back to the city. He used to bring me anywhere—to all the teen clubs. He would have brought me to the moon if I would have asked him.

At the church, I was at the back. I could see Rachel through the crowd. When a man started singing, I started crying. I cried all the way out the church. I couldn't do nothing but cry. My cousin Roi came and hugged me and said, "It's gonna be all good, don't trip." I was speechless. They carried him out of the church and into the hearse and my cousin took pictures. We second lined through the torn down project to the gym. It must have been a hundred degrees outside. We danced and took pictures. I was with Bee's brother George and his cousin Cory. Then Abram called and said, "We comin."

I knew Bee for six years, eight months, 30 minutes, and 5,256 seconds. He was my step-daddy. He showed me how to ride a bike, fight—all kinds of things. When I got to that age, he showed me how to drive. Bee always knew how to make you feel good.

Brandon's casket, by Pernell Russell.

Interview with My Mom, Part IV

Mother.

I asked my mom to tell me about she felt about losing Brandon.

Pernell: How did you feel about having a baby with Bee?

Tica: It was a blessing to have a baby for my honey, but not to have a baby for my honey when he's not here—when he's gone. That's not a happy picture, there. It's hard. We always talked about, "We're gonna have a baby." I liked how he used to be with you and your brothers. He was mature for his age. He was the type of man who would be a good role model. He finished school, he was in college, and he had a job. He just had his head on his shoulders at a young age.

Pernell: What is the best memory of him that you have?

Tica: A lot of them—there's not one set memory. But I always think about him for Katrina. He chose to stay with us and make sure we were straight. That's what I loved about him. Even though we used to be together on and off, we still had this sticky glue bond where if it's gonna help you or hurt, I'm gonna tell him, and he's gonna tell me.

Pernell: How did you feel about losing him?

Tica: That's a feeling right there that's unexplainable cause you never stop hurting. I'm still going through something that I'm not over yet. That's something that could drive you crazy if you ain't a strong person. It can fuck your whole world up. It really could. It sets your mind in whole other place. Have you forget about reality. They still haven't found who killed my honey yet.

Brandon's repass, by Pernell Russell.

Pernell (Doo), Block, T-Tiga, and Roi Lowrey at Brandon's repass wearing his memorial t-shirt, courtesy of the Russell family.

More Bad News

Justin's mom, Christine, called me. She asked for my mama. I said, "Hold on," and gave my mama the phone and whatever Justin's mama said made my mama freeze up. I knew something was wrong from the look in her eye. The eyes never lie.

She turned around and closed the door by the kitchen so I couldn't hear. My mama came behind me and said, "Bae, Justin dead." I said, "How he died?"

"Christine said he got shot. His brother Robert found him in her backyard. Robert started going crazy. Ran in the street with a bat and said he was gonna kill somebody behind his brother."

I said to myself, "Shit, it's for real." I started having flashbacks and then I went into one of those moments where I don't want to talk to anybody.

R.I.P. Jay

Pernell and Tica, by Rachel Breunlin.

August 27, 2008. 7:30 pm

-Times-Picayune

A man was shot Wednesday night and found dead in a spot not far from an Algiers apartment complex where – according to neighborhood residents – shots were fired weeks ago in the air and in the ground "just for fun."

The man, who did not have any identification on him, was pronounced dead at the scene, said Officer Jonette Williams, a New Orleans Police Department spokeswoman. The shooting occurred about 7:30 p.m., she said, and his body, with a gunshot wound to the torso, was found in the backyard of a home in the 1500 block of Murl Street.

Police late Wednesday had no motive or suspects.

Christopher Smith, 17, said he led police to the body who he said was Justin Laird.

Smith said he attended school with Laird's brother, at O. Perry Walker High School in Algiers.

Cedric Laird, who described himself as an uncle of the deceased, said Justin did not attend school, but the teenager spent a lot of time with his pregnant girlfriend and her 1-year-old daughter from another relationship.

Cedric Laird, said he was on his computer, when he heard several shots. Laird said he moved into the neighborhood in January and recently witnessed a small group of people in the Gilmore Park apartment complex, part of which fenced off by razor wire, shooting a gun in the air and in the ground "for no reason."

He said he called the police to report the incident, but the police didn't find the weapon.

"It's always been a problem with the guys who live there," Laird said.

A woman who lives across the street from the complex said she too had seen someone fire a handgun in the air and into the ground, once when "there were children around."

Interview with Roi Lowrey *cousin,*

After Justin and Brandon passed, I stopped dancing, stopped making clothes, and didn't even skateboard as much. I just felt like hanging with my friends that I grew up with in the St. Bernard. We formed a group called Sigel Street.

Let me tell about the gang: Roi Lowrey—he was all about girls until he met T-Baby, his girlfriend. Hank's a football player. Raheem Fresh is always fresh. T-Tiga is a basketball player. Melvin: one word, gangsta. Cayoonie is a football player for 35 known all over the state. Then there's Dee-Dee Bipolar and then there's me, Doo Neno. I think of Pernell as the positive side of me. He is respectable, but let somebody make me mad and that's when I turn into Doo Neno.

When he comes out, I don't care. I don't want to hear nothin. That's why I came up with the name Doo Neno da Gunna. I'm trying to change, but it's like every time I change a little, something happens and Doo Neno comes out.

Sigel started this thing with our hand—you stick your middle finger and your pinky up and fold the rest down. We made our own sign. Then Roi Lowrey was like, "We need a name for ourselves." That's when he said, "Sigel Street." I felt I should have interviewed him because he's a big inspiration to me in lots of ways. He has his wisdom right.

Roi Lowrey, by Pernell Russell.

Pernell: What's Sigel Street?

Roi: Lifetime friends. It was something that was in the St. Bernard Project. A lot of the different cliques were named after Def Jam and the Roc-A-Fella label.

Sigel Street is another clique. At first we were Bad Ass Children (BAC) and then we changed our name to The St. Bernard Mob (SBM). Now we're Sigel Street, which we named ourselves after Beanie Sigel. Sigel Street is often called out in his raps. That's final. It's not going to change.

Pernell: How do you decide who was going to be in Sigel Street?

Roi: We don't recruit that often. If we do, it's somebody who is close to us. We're not a gang, and we don't accept followers. Everyone has to have their own mind, but also be part of the group. Basically, you have be you—you have to have pride, heart, and confidence.

Pernell: You've got to have swag. It's the way you carry yourself.

Roi: And the outfit just puts the icing on the cake.

Pernell: What would you call not having swag?

Roi: Anybody who's not in style. Some things are just inappropriate to wear, like Reebok Classics. This isn't 1994, son. People like that make our name look bad.

THE .45 gun

Pernell: Tell me a story when we were all together.

Roi: We had came from a boring Sweet 16 party. When we came home, you had the gun. It was a .45. You were like, "Everybody gonna get a chance to shoot the gun." We were like, "All right, yeah."

But then I thought about it. If you shoot it, it's not going to be long before the police come. So not all of us would be able to shoot. When we got to the train tracks, we were all like, "Don't shoot it right here."

Pernell: I didn't want to hear that.

Roi: And all the sudden: *Bow bow bow bow bow!!* I was right there next to you while you was shooting. Everyone else was gone. All we saw was their backs. They left us. While we were walking back we said, "Don't take that way cause if the police see them we don't want to be following them." When we went up the street, we saw the police coming down the street with the sirens.

Pernell: They turned back the other way, and we were hiding in an abandoned backyard. They had this dog in another yard and it kept barking at us, so we had to hide from the dog! You were like, "Put the gun under the house!" I kept saying, "No! I ain't gonna leave my gun." We were arguing for a good five minutes, until I just left the gun and we ran to my house. Everybody was like "Man, you fake."

Roi: Because he wouldn't let them shoot the gun.

A WILD THING

Pernell: Where does Sigel Street go on the weekends?

Roi: It depends on what's poppin for the weekend. If they don't have no parties, we're going to Bourbon later that night.

Pernell: And what y'all do on Bourbon?

Roi: If it's on Bourbon, we'll probably get drunk. When you're drunk, some truths comes out. One time, we had a fight with the people on the balcony, throwing beads and cups at them. We were having fun but, you know, it was a wild thing. Teenagers do a lot of wild things.

Pernell: What about the time when the people were beating on buckets?

Roi: I was looking at them and thought, "Let me go do that." People were dropping change and I was beating on drums. It was a wild night.

FASHION

Pernell: What were people wearing when we were young and how did the fashion change?

Roi: I would say that was that Iceberg stuff, the platinum clothing, and jerseys.

Pernell: And how did the fashion change?

Roi: It went from that to Rocawear and Sean John, and then now it goes to everything. Now it's Hollister—any type of thing. Everybody got their own style now. It's not designer labels. Everybody got their own style.

Pernell: How did you get involved in fashion?

Roi: My brother, Matt, is involved in a clothing line and he showed me all these urban web sites on the internet. You are going to have people listening to this interview, right? I can't say which ones because then lame people might go to them. And then there are boutiques and they retail clothes. One's in the French Quarter. It's called Traffic Boutique.

Pernell: And do you think you ever want to pursue being a fashion designer?

Roi: I'm trying to right now. I'm in the Fashion Institute of New Orleans. I think they have that at your school. I'm designing clothes and creating my own line. I'm going to call it Roi Lowrey—I'm making clothes for women.

Pernell: Why are you going to make clothes for women?

Roi: Because women are the biggest shoppers in the world. [*Laughter*] They live in the mall—they've got to look good no matter what.

When All the Action Happens

One day Roi Lowrey called me and said they had this girl write him on MySpace. He showed her to me and I was like, "No, I don't know her." The next day at school, I walked into class, and she was in there. I just heard a voice say, "You that boy who be with Roi and them." From that day, we started being cool.

The next day at school, she sat by me for breakfast. She said, "I want to be with Sigel." I called everybody on the phone and said, "Ebbie want to be our First Lady." They all said "Iight!!!" That's how she got in.

On the weekends, we acted like we were a mafia. We went to my house to watch for nightfall like vampires. Night is when all the action happens. Henry kept talking about his school dance so we was headed to Edna Karr. They were checking us like we were going to see the president.

The dance was so hot, the floor was sweating. Dudes were dancing, showing off their shoulder work and footwork. I did not even want to look behind me because I knew the whole Sigel was looking at me to dance. When I turned around they were saying, "Go ahead."

I started shoulder working and foot working, holding onto the wall until I saw Monte.

I said, "Oh yeah, some shakers." Monte spotted me and said, "Doo, you ready?"

I said, "You already know."

Soon as we started dancing, he got on the floor. I took advantage of that because he couldn't really do many moves in that position on the floor. When we finished, we started teaming together and burnt everybody til it was over. When we got home, we all got on the phone with each other. I called T-Tiga, and he called Roi Lowrey on three way. Roi called Raheem Fresh, Raheem called Hank, and Hank called Melvin, who called Ebbie, then Ebbie called three-way to Cayoonie and Cayoonie called Dee Dee to recount the night nine ways.

Terrance "T-Tiga" Alford, by Pernell Russell.

Days with T-Tiga

T-Tiga and I are together every day. We only live three blocks from each other. When I get off my school bus, he's already at my house and he always has a story. Like, "Son, I got me a cool chick at school today." Or, "Guess who I was about to fight?" Then we always go to the store to get our snacks and start our daily rounds. We walk through the whole Eighth Ward messing with people and stopping by all Tiga's girls. We stop by Melvin's house on Roman and Marigny to talk, get two of the dogs and let them run around for about an hour, then give them some water in the backyard of my house.

While the dogs are in the back, I'll get on the phone while T-Tiga fixes us Hot Pockets—we can't live without our Hot Pockets—and then he'll watch *Boyz in the Hood* over and over. After a few hours, T-Tiga will say, "I'm bored, let's bring the dogs back." On our walks, we always end up talking about Sigel Street. As it starts to get dark, Tiga says, "I'm about to home before eight o'clock."

I might say, "You scary," but then we walk each other half way home, dap hands and say, "Call me, son."

I'm Right Here

Ebbie and I got closer and closer until we started to call each other brotha and sista. She put me on her MySpace page and I put her on mine. One day at school, my cousin Dee Dee said, "Doo, guess who like you?"

"Who?"

"Ebbie."

"My sis?"

"Yeah, Ebbie said she think you're cute."

That night on the phone I said, "Guess what?"

"What?"

I told her, "I used to like you," when I really wanted to say, "I like you."

Ebbie went everywhere with Sigel Street. She was like one of the guys until one day I said, "Fuck it." I had a plan. T-Tiga came by my house and I said, "Do this for me. Call Ebbie and play like I'm not around and tell her I like her." Tiga called Ebbie and I was right there listening.

I went home and called her, playing it off by saying, "What's up, sis?" She said, "I heard something about you."

"What?" I was laughing and sort of nervous on the inside.

"T-Tiga said you like me."

"He down bad. I told him not to tell nobody that."

"Don't trip, I like you, too."

"What you want to do about the situation? I'ma be your Doo Neno and you be my Ebbie."

As soon as I said that, she started being quiet. We did not know what to say, we were so used to being sis and bro.

That day came. She came by my house. We were watching BET and started wrestling. When I fell on top of her, we kissed. We got that stupid look on our face like, "What just happened?"

Out of the blue, I said, "Let's go to the store." We were walking in the street and Ebbie said, "You think you got bumpers?"

"No, why?"

"Cause you in the middle of the street!"

When we got to the store, I said, "You want something?"

She said, "Yeah," in a shy way.

I bought some cold drinks and went back to my house. I said, "Let's go inside." I closed the doors to my room and she went to the bathroom. When she came back, I had turned off the lights.

"Why you sitting in the dark?"

"I'm just thinking."

"What you thinking about?"

"You."

She said, "I'm right here."

My Grandma Was a Big Figure in the Hood

I was asleep and it was raining. I got a phone call from Duke, my auntie's boyfriend. He said, "Your grandma just got shot." I was still asleep and said, "Stop playing." Then Melvin's baby mama Samantha called crying, saying, "Doo, they shot her."

I jumped out of the bed and said, "Fuck!" I called T-Tiga and I got two of my handguns. He pulled up, and we drove over to my grandma's house on New Orleans Street. When I saw all the flashing lights, I went into a rage, wanting to kill any and everything.

I tried to go on my grandma's porch, but the police told me to stand back a whole block. The ambulance rode off and I thought she was going to make it. Ten minutes later, I got the worst phone call of my life. She didn't make it.

I was in silence the whole day—I mean complete silence. All I wanted was a name. Just give me a name.

Every day until my grandma's funeral people from the project gathered at her house on New Orleans Street with DJs and barbecue. One day they were DJing and the police came and told my uncle, "Go inside." My uncle told him, "I'm a grown man." The police said, "Grow your bitch ass inside." We took the DJ speakers inside and kept partying and barbecuing and the police stood in front of my grandmother's door like they were waiting for us to come out.

The big day came. I woke up to my mama doing my brother's hair. I did everything you're supposed to do when you wake up and when I got dressed my uncle Cino came. When we got there, my mother, her sister, Melvin, and Kelvin got out of the limousine. The church was packed. They made my whole family march in two-by-two holding hands. As I was marching in, I saw Rachel, Lea, and little Max in the crowd. They were the only white people there.

As we were sitting in the pews, I saw my grandmother laying there. Melvin was behind me. I was trying to hold my laughing in, but he kept whispering jokes. But once they called the final verse and we went up to the casket, he broke down. My friend Henry kept saying, "It's going to be all right, son," over and over.

They carried my grandma to the hearse. When we were driving to the graveyard, 50 cars were following us. It was the last time I saw her.

Shrine in honor of Maggie Russell where she was shot, by Pernell Russell.

Interview with Edward Buckner, Part II

Ed and Pernell on Ed's porch, by Abram Himelstein.

I'm 17 now. I feel like I'm becoming a man. I'm trying to grow up but it's hard when I don't have my father around very much. I try to tell myself I don't need my dad, I got my mama, Sigel Street, myself. I want to be somebody. I don't want to be another bum-ass person who is not trying to do anything with themselves.

Guns took away my step-daddy Brandon, my friend Justin, and my grandmother. She died helping someone. It was raining and she tried to give a man an umbrella, and a man shot them. Brandon was like another father. Someone killed him over a fight in a club.

I have thought of revenge, but if I would have killed them, it would have kept the cycle going. I would have killed them, someone would have killed me, then one of my people would have killed them. I'm not trying to live like that on the run, can't go to this place and that place because I have to watch my back.

I wanted to ask Ed what it was like to lose Brandon and not go crazy. I wanted to know how you deal with that pain and stay positive, how you represent your hood without contributing to the beef—the jealousy, feuds, and violence. I don't want to forget the St. Bernard, but I don't want to be stuck in the past. I'm just trying to find my light at the end of the tunnel—hopefully through school and this book.

Pernell: What kind of relationship do me and you have?

Ed: You're like my son, boy. You're my people. You know what kind of relationship we have, I love you, you love me. I know that. You're family.

Pernell: What are some of your dreams?

Ed: My dream is that no young men and young women would die from gunfire. That we could find a way to get along. My dream is that the world could find a bright light to shine on a community like this one despite all the neglect and challenges it has been through. My dream's that kids don't go hungry. Or that I could call the music stores in New Orleans and they would decide to give me instruments to help these young boys.

I don't want them to sell drugs. I don't want them to shoot anybody. I don't want them to be criminal minded—stealing, snatching purses. If I can put that horn in their mouth, teach them some notes and some songs to play, they might go down to the French Quarters one day and be a Kermit Ruffins, a

Left: Ed with his children: Toye, Samantha, and Brandon. *Right:* Taylor, Ed's youngest daughter with his wife, Nakia. Photographs courtesy of the Buckner family.

Kidd Jordan, Jelly Roll Morton, Trombone Shorty.

I think my dream is just that we as people and not just black people, but white, Mexicans, and just everybody could melt together. We melt only for minutes and we break apart and are crazy again. I dream that white women like Rachel can work with black boys like you and we can find great gathering points. That we are making great strides as people, instead of people thinking, "What that white lady might be using you for," and "You better not like that white lady." To take away the prejudice of things. To know she has something to teach to you, and you have a lot to teach to her.

I believe at the end of the day—I might not be living to see it—but it's going to be all good. All this will be good. All my hard work will never be in vain. All of our kids will be able to cross North Claiborne Avenue and play with kids over here and kids over on the other side will be their friends. And we won't have anything like the Prieur Columbus Boys and the Frenchman and Villere boys and all the other rivalries that destroys us as a body of people.

BRANDON

Brandon's mama was my John McDonogh high school sweetheart. We parted when he was about three years old, but I would get every summer with Bee. I had these nice apartments in the East and Bee would swim all day throughout the whole summer.

It was just that special bond that we had. For me, being such a young, young, baby daddy with a little bitty baby, we grew together. Through all my ill moments, he just saw his daddy. He was the youngest of all the boys in the family, and he was really competitive, but he did what I wanted him to do. He was a man that handled schoolwork. He graduated—that was a proud crowning moment to me. He started going to college and made the baby, Brandy. He got to be

Lil Troy, whose father introduced Tica and Brandon, plays at Brandis' first birthday party, sixth months after Brandon was murdered. Troy is a part of the Big Seven Brass Band, which Ed manages. Photograph by Lea Downing.

a junior, and I'm thinking, "We're ready to go now." And for him to tragically lose his life so soon after he had the new baby, Brandis, that's a ball of fire there.

I tried to make his funeral be a time that totally reflected on him, even through my moments when I was wanting to break down or jump out the church window and run away. Second line parades was his thing. I tell you, if he wouldn't have died, he would have paraded with the rest of my children. I didn't get a chance to do that with him, but I felt like we celebrated the day of the parade because it was only like a week or two after Bee's death. That whole day

I had people coming to me saying, "B-boy right here with you. Do your thing for your baby. This the time for you and your baby, just let it all off now. Get all that off you from what happened."

Pernell: Remember the night he wrecked that PT Cruiser? He came to my house and he told me he saw his whole life flash.

Ed: He told me that, too.

Pernell: He said he wanted us to walk him through the St. Bernard, and he wanted us to lift his casket up seven times.

Ed: Where the parade first went by was a blue building—it was a grocery store—right in that area is where myself and Brandon all grew up. You and your family right there in that area, too. I'll never forget your great- grandma, Ms. Lily Rose, and other women like Ms. Shirley Moss, Ms. Shirley Bob, Ms. Angelique. Brandon wanted to play with BB guns and I would buy them for him, being a dumb young daddy. They would catch him with that gun and run him home. Take the gun and every-thing! And you don't look at it til I got older that those people helped raise my children.

I used to tell him, "Bee, you are the blueprint. You're my oldest boy, so if I get you through college, all the rest of them have to follow." The kid who killed him, killed my blueprint. I was able to forgive him. I don't know who he is, never seen him, never heard of him, but I was able to find strength in my heart and through my God to take and find a way to forgive him. He destroyed a life and traumatized my family so bad, but his life has to have changed, too. You go from this free man to a running man, paranoid, wondering if one of my family members might turn the bend hoping to kill you.

He doesn't know I went to my family and told them I don't need them taking another life. I don't need this snowballing. I need this to end now. One of the first things I told you in this interview—just stop young men from taking up arms against each other and kill-ing one another. Many of you have so much prom-ise—so much talent in your hands and brains—and to kill one another off at this rate, it's just dangerous not only to us as a black people, but to all the chil-dren to come.

Ed with the Big Seven Brass Band in front of Pernell's house for Brandis' birthday party. Photograph by Lea Downing.

We've got to find conflict resolution skills. We've got to find the things that bring our community back to-gether once an incident happens. It starts from the leadership in the community. The St. Bernard Project is a reflection of all of our family's community.

The buildings being torn down hurts, but it doesn't take away from the spirit of the land and the people who walk that land—day in and day out. The fami-lies who have come through before Brandon and my-self and the families who will go after us will walk around, and they will say, "This is where my mama came up at." Or, "This is where my daddy came up at." The buildings might not be there, but the spirit will continue. I don't care what you build on it, it will never be anything different.

Jave and Pernell dancing at Brandis' birthday party, by Lea Downing.

Portrait of Brandon on display at Ed's house along with other
family photographs, by Abram Himelstein.

NSP AFTERWORD

December 2009

It has been a long four years for the Neighborhood Story Project since the last series of books by John McDonogh students came out. In June of 2005, we were riding high, with five books by high school students circulating the city and neighborhoods were they were written. After Harry Potter, they were the best sellers in the city.

And in August of 2005 we were back at John McDonogh, with 60 applicants for the next round of book-making, and went home for a weekend of sorting applications. On Monday, the levees failed, and the applications were waiting on Rachel's kitchen table when we got back to town seven weeks later, a grim reminder of one more thing lost.

The NSP set about the work it knew, making books with Nine Times Social and Pleasure Club, making posters about the Seventh Ward, and a book of community gathering spots- Cornerstones. But through it all we wanted to go back to John McDonogh and hear what was happening in teenage-land.

So in the fall of 2007, we went recruiting at John Mac. We were holding the first round of books, relics of the pre-storm era, and very few of the new students had heard of them. There were five brave souls who signed up for a class in book-making. Daron Crawford, Susan Henry, Kareem Kennedy, Kenneth Phillips, and Pernell Russell.

The first part was the easiest. We read the first round of NSP books and the classics like: *Life and Death on the South Side of Chicago*, and Sherman Alexie's *Lone Ranger and Tonto First Fight in Heaven*.

And then we started on the two and a half year journey of writing our stories. We wrote about life before Katrina, and some of the Katrina experience, but we mostly worked on Documenting the Now.

The Now was ever-changing: Daron moved from house to house, and studio to studio. Kareem went from high school student to Delgado student. Pernell went from nearly care-free (dancing, making clothes) to dealing with loss. Susan's career in fashion and cosmetology went from theoretical to real. Kenneth worked on his anger management, while getting learning about his past.

We began to talk about the need to have something at stake in the book- the need to represent our struggles and not just the things that we wanted people to know about our lives. Or as Kareem Kennedy put it to everyone, "People want to read your mind to ease their mind."

And so we started in on the writing the hard parts. We went to where the projects were in the process of being torn down. Sneaking in through holes in fences, we roamed where the thousands lived, now desolate and post-apocalyptic. We went to the new spaces, shotgun doubles, ranch homes in the suburbs, and we wrote to make sense of the changes.

Rachel taught interviewing and ethnography- how to de-familiarize yourself with your surroundings and connect your personal stories to the larger cultures of New Orleans. Abram taught writing styles. Lea and Lindsey went with the writers to interview and photograph.

During 2008 we kept at it, interviewing family, former neighbors, other people who could help broaden their perspectives on themes in the books.

In March of 2008 the NSP published *The House of Dance and Feathers: A Museum by Ronald Lewis*, and the writers got to see their first NSP book release party- in Ronald's backyard in the Lower Ninth Ward, Mardi Gras Indians and Brass Bands. Two hundred people dancing in the rain.

As Rachel turned her attention from editing *The House of Dance and Feathers*, toward working on building up the structures of the four books the work kicked into overdrive. Weekends became an abstract idea, as writers and NSP staff started to live in our office in Seventh Ward. We took occasional breaks to go back out and get more photos, or to get the interviewees more involved in the editing process.

In September of 2009 we printed out what we had and gave copies to family and friends and impartial readers. They came together as book committees, telling us what they liked and what the books needed to feel finished. We took notes, gave ourselves a weekend off, and then got back on the horse.

October was the end of the road. We had to weigh what pieces stayed in, how to tell the untold parts. Hard decisions as the idea of books met the reality of paper and print. Late nights and early mornings led to this- four new books, five new authors, and a return to the roots of the NSP.

NSP'S HUGE LIST OF THANK-YOUS

Our first and biggest thank-you to our authors and their families: Daron Crawford, Susan Henry, Kareem Kennedy, Kenneth Phillips, and Pernell Russell. It has been two great years of getting to know y'all, and a huge honor to be so involved in your lives. We are proud of your work, and feel blessed to have become family. We look forward to knowing y'all and reading y'all for years to come.

To the mighty University of New Orleans—the College of Liberal Arts, the College of Education, and UNO Press: We are grateful and proud to be a part of the University community. Thank you to Chancellor Ryan, Susan Krantz, Rick Barton, Bob Cashner, Joe King, and Anthony Cipolone. In Anthropology, thank you to David Beriss, Jeffrey Ehrenreich, and Martha Ward. In the College of Education, thank you to Jim Meza, Andre Perry, and April Whatley Bedford. At UNO Press, Bill Lavender and GK Darby.

To all the people who have supported the NSP, thank you. Huge gratitude to all of the writers at the write-a-thon, without whom we could not have made this milestone. We look forward to out-writing last year's amazingness.

To the Lupin Foundation. Thank you for your consistent support over the years. These books could not have happened without you.

To our John McDonogh Senior High/ RSD family—Principal Gerald Debose, Antoinette Pratcher, Dawn Greay, Alicia Carter Watts, Shawon Bernard, Brother Jamal Robertson, Deborah Richardson, Nira Cooper and all of the other teachers at the Mac. Thank you for working with us and for being so supportive of the efforts of the NSP.

Thank you to the Cowan Family and Jewish Funds for Justice. Your gift kept us going, and Paul's legacy continues to inspire us.

To Gareth, thank you for going above and beyond, once again, to balance a crazy amount of work with beautiful design.

For getting us ready to go to press, Felicia McCarren, Jordan Flaherty, Siobhan Flahive McKieran, Ariella Cohen, GK Darby, Bill Lavender, Hot Iron Press, and Eve Abrams.

To the Bard Early College in New Orleans program and Stephen Tremaine: thank you for being an awesome partner in this work.

To our board—Petrice Sams Abiodun, Susan Krantz. Corlita Mahr Spreen, Troy Materre, Helen Regis, and Emelda Wylie. It has been a great journey with y'all, and we are looking forward to more.

Thank you to the Zeitoun Foundation for supporting the work. Your unsolicited gift was a huge boost to our organization, and your story of reclaiming against great odds has been part of our inspiration.

And to our families: Dan and Max Omar Etheridge; Cynthia Breunlin, Doug Breunlin and Nanci Gordon, Megan Etheridge, and Kate, Tommaso, and Zoe Weichmann (for stepping in to help take care of Rachel's men while she was on editing lockdown); Nolan Marshall, Tessa Corthell, Shana Sassoon, Phyllis, Linda and Jerry, the Hsiangs, the Downings, the Darnells: thank you for being our family through this process. We could not have done it without you, and we are glad we didn't have to try.

Viva New Orleans

Rachel Breunlin, Lindsey Darnell, Lea Downing and Abram Himelstein

Neighborhood Story Project